Something Good
for Those Who Feel Bad

Something Good for Those Who Feel Bad

Positive Solutions for Negative Emotions

Louis O. Caldwell

BAKER BOOK HOUSE
Grand Rapids, Michigan 49506

Some of these chapters originally appeared in pamphlet form under the titles *You Can Develop a Positive Self-Image* © 1984; *You Can Face Suffering* © 1978; *You Can Find Help Through Counseling* © 1983; *You Can Overcome Discouragement* © 1983; *You Can Overcome Your Fears, Phobias, and Worries* © 1985; *You Can Prevent or Overcome a Nervous Breakdown* © 1978; *You Can Stop Feeling Guilty* © 1978.

Unless otherwise indicated, Scripture references are from the King James Version of the Bible. Other translations used are the American Revised Version (ARV), the Living Bible (LB), The Bible: A New Translation by James Moffatt (*Moffat*), the New English Bible (NEB), the New International Version (NIV), the New Testament in Modern English (*Phillips*), and the Revised Standard Version (RSV).

To

my clients
who have learned
in counseling that
he is the way, the truth,
and the life.

Contents

Introduction

While writing this book, I thought back over thirty years of counseling people who were seeking help. This ministry has been exercised in a variety of places: homes, schools, summer camps, seminars, hospitals, jails, and churches, as well as in the consulting room in my private practice.

My notes and memory are filled with what these hurting persons most frequently say to me. One thing they all have in common is that they feel bad. They commonly describe their negative emotions with such statements as "I feel terrible," "weak," "rotten," "low," "blue," "empty," "fragmented," "lost," "lonely," "stuck," "inferior," "worthless," "ugly," or "abnormal." They commonly use phrases such as "coming apart," "brokenhearted," "soul sick," "full of fear, hostility, jealousy, guilt." And it's probably safe to say that such are the emotional states of each of us at one time or another.

These emotional conditions can be so miserable and painful that we are intensely motivated to do something—sometimes anything—to eliminate or at least reduce the inner torment. When the solution is negative, it can take all-too-familiar forms: use of drugs or alcohol, sickness, sexual promiscuity, lawlessness, obsessive-compulsive behavior, social withdrawal, even suicide.

It is appalling to consider the scope, magnitude, and depth of human suffering caused by wrong, sinful, or foolish ways of attempting to change how we feel. The bitter results take tragically familiar forms: families torn apart, jobs lost, friendships destroyed, projects abandoned, potential wasted.

In this book, I have focused on those emotional problems for which my clients have most frequently sought help. I fully realize that my treatment of the topics is limited, primarily because of the complex nature of our feelings. The garment of the emotional life is a Joseph's coat of many colors, the differences often being in degree rather than kind.

I believe that you can explain the course and quality of most people's lives according to what they do to feel good, and what they do when they feel bad. Our stability, our sense of wholeness, our sense of aliveness, peace, and power is related to this inner world of feeling. We do well, therefore, to understand it better—its mystery, complexity, variability, rhythms, and force.

Without denying the importance of sound research and recorded human experience, I am convinced that we must have the Bible as our guide if we are to understand ourselves and find acceptable solutions for our emotional problems. Recently a middle-aged man in Denver, Colorado, told me that he was about to enter a mental institution when he read the chapter about nervous breakdowns. The scriptural interpretation and solution of the problem helped him to regain his mental and emotional health. Today he is living a productive, joyful life. He experienced the evidence that "all Scripture is God-breathed" (2 Tim. 3:16, NIV).

My purpose in writing this book is to attempt to interpret the meaning of the gospel in connection with our emotions. The word *gospel* means "good news," and we need to know that the news is good when our feelings are bad! Jesus said, "I have come that they might have life, and that they might have it more abundantly" (John 10:10). That abundant life can be ours, no matter how we feel. Moreover, inherent in that abundant life are positive strategies and adequate resources for dealing with our negative emotions.

I wish to express my deepest gratitude to those who have helped me in the preparation of this manuscript: Mary Lee Evans (who accepted most of the secretarial work), Joycelyn Clairmonte, and my sister Sally Clark for their deciphering and typing skills, to my editor, Dan Van't Kerkhoff, for the book's title, and to Bobbi Spurgeon, versatile and gifted helper who proofread the manuscript.

In addition, I owe a great debt of gratitude to Drs. Charles L. Allen, J. Wallace Hamilton, Norman Vincent Peale, Robert Schuller, and Leslie Weatherhead—preachers whose books continue to help and inspire; to Drs. La Verne Carmical and J. Don Boney—professors in the graduate school of the University of Houston who led me to a deeper understanding of troubled people; and to Dr. Paul Tournier, Christian physician and therapist, whose books pioneered for me an integration of theology, philosophy, and psychology.

1

Dealing with Negative Emotions

In a demonstration on the West Coast, someone observed a demonstrator carrying a poster with this intriguing message:

> Jesus Christ is the answer;
> what's the question?

A short time later in another demonstration, someone carried a placard that read:

> Is there life after birth?

Quite a question, isn't it! It focuses on our deepest need. We want *life*—not more days in our lives, but more life in our days. Perhaps no generation has ever asked more urgently than ours, "Is there life after birth?"

Phillip James Bailey had experience on his side when he wrote: "We live in deeds, not years; in thoughts, not breaths; in feelings, not figures on a dial. We should count time by heart throbs. He most lives who thinks most, feels the noblest, acts the best." We are not satisfied merely to live. If given the choice between quantity of life and quality of life, most of us would not hesitate to choose quality. How long we live does not matter as much as how well we live. We share with Henry David Thoreau the dread of approaching death only to discover "that I had not lived." He "wanted to live deep and suck

out all the marrow of life." And in our moments of clearest thinking, so do we.

Because this sense of aliveness expresses itself most
forcefully in the way we feel, we learn to place great
importance on our emotions. Some would go as far as
John Ruskin, who said, "The ennobling difference between one man and another...is precisely this, that one
feels more than another."

You can easily observe our society's emphasis on emotion in our manner of greeting each other. "How are you
feeling?" we commonly ask. At times this question brings
answers that make us wish we'd avoided the subject entirely! For example, a minister came home late. "Where
have you been for the last two hours?" demanded his
wife. "I met Mrs. Brown at the store and asked her how
she was feeling," sighed the weary pastor.

I have been a better-informed husband since a client
shared this insight: "A woman may forget what happened to her twenty years ago, but she will always remember how she felt about it!"

Another example of our society's emphasis on emotion
is our expression of opinion. "I feel that we ought to
make that change," or "It's my feeling that people don't
think things through," or "They felt that they were
right" are commonly-heard expressions.

One reason for this emphasis on emotion can be
found in our society's headlong plunge into computeri-
zation, mechanization, and standardization. To counteract this trend, we must be reminded at regular intervals
what wholeness and health and being human really
mean. The price we pay in an increasing sense of deper-
sonalization is a fearful one. We don't have to sacrifice
competency to feel compassion, and perfection without
passion soon loses its appeal. The revival of a striving
for excellence that we are seeing in our nation's corpo-
rate life is promising, provided that along with excel-

lence we're not deprived of excitement. A society bereft of inspiration, energy, and robust emotional life cannot indefinitely sustain its intellectual performance.

In an era boasting of its scientific achievements and intellectual attainments, should we think seriously about emotion? Or have we become so educated that we no longer understand that "the heart has its reasons of which reason knows nothing; we feel it in many things"? Blaise Pascal, in his classic work, *Pensées*, explains further: "Reason acts slowly, with so much deliberation and on so many principles (which must always be present) that it is constantly falling asleep, or going astray for want of having all its principles present. Feeling does not act thus, but instantaneously, and it is ever ready to act" (p. 3). Better than most, Pascal understood that reason functions in relationship to the heart and that our feelings have a profound effect on the rational mind. He went so far as to state: "All our reasoning amounts to no more than giving way to feeling. . . . Reason can be made to serve any purpose" (p. 1).

Our Emotions and Our Health

In *None of These Diseases*, Dr. S. I. McMillen, a Christian physician, gives a striking explanation of the influence of our emotions on our physical health. He notes that the emotional center is located in the brain; from it nerve fibers go out to every organ of the body. Any "turmoil in the emotional center" can send out impulses through the intricate nerve connections. Emotional stress thus can be a factor in diseases or disorders ranging from ulcers, high blood pressure, heart disease, and strokes to headaches, backaches, allergies, and infections.

Many of my clients have asked how emotions can produce such a variety of physical problems. This occurs in three ways:

1. by changing the amount of blood flowing to an organ
2. by affecting the secretions of certain glands
3. by changing the tension of muscles

Dr. William Sadler believed that only a medical doctor can fully appreciate the "amazingly large amounts of human disease and suffering" caused by worry, fear, conflict, immorality, dissipation, ignorance, unwholesome thinking, and unclean living.

However, centuries before modern medicine and psychiatry, students of the Bible understood the cause of many of our psychosomatic problems. "The activities of the lower nature are obvious. Here is a list: sexual immorality, . . . hatred, quarreling, jealousy, bad temper, rivalry, factions, party spirit, envy, drunkenness, . . . and things like that" (Gal. 5:19–21, *Phillips*).

Beyond the diagnosis is the cure. "Those who belong to Christ Jesus have crucified the flesh with its emotions and passions" (Gal. 5:24, *Moffatt*). To quote Sadler, "The sincere acceptance of the principles and teachings of Christ with respect to the life of mental peace and joy, the life of unselfish thought and clean living, would at once wipe out more than half the difficulties, disease and sorrows of the human race."*

Emotion and Past Experience

Our emotions not only respond to what we're experiencing in the present, but also can release a delayed reaction to what we experienced in the past. In this regard we are much like the dachshund which Dr. L. O. Smith of the University of Chicago describes:

---

*William Sadler, *Practice of Psychiatry* (Saint Louis: C. V. Mosby, 1953), p. 1008.

He hadn't any notion
How long it took to notify
His tail of his emotion;
And so it happened, while his eyes
Were filling with woe and sadness,
His little tail went wagging on
Because of previous gladness.

Most of us fail to appreciate the cumulative effect of our thoughts, feelings, and behavior. What we think about, feel, and do because of the pattern of living we choose makes the beds that we must lie in.

Emotional pain can be especially difficult for adolescents and adults to handle when its origin is in traumatic experiences in childhood. The death of a parent (especially the mother), physical abuse, emotional abuse, sexual abuse, and serious illness are the leading childhood traumas. Other emotionally disturbing experiences in childhood include parental neglect, the death of a sibling or best friend, a broken home or one where there is constant conflict, or frequent changes in schools and neighborhoods.

These experiences are as powerful as they are painful. They can also trigger a variety of responses in adulthood, when intimate relationships are formed. Intimacy, by its very nature, involves the emotions. And when the emotional fuse is lighted by the present linking itself with a troubled past, the explosion can shatter the personality. Emotions such as fear, grief, guilt, shame, and rage can be overwhelming, especially when the person cannot understand their origins. Reactions can take several forms, confusion, distrust, depression, and withdrawal being among the most common. In addition, there are symptoms such as nightmares, anxiety attacks, and numerous psychosomatic reactions.

These kinds of emotional problems block personality growth, interfere with interpersonal relationships, and can even hinder a person in developing a relationship to God. Such problems will not go away with the passing of time. In fact, these kind of problems tend to get worse as time passes. "Time heals all wounds" is a popular saying that cannot be applied to these kinds of wounds. But when the cause is identified, understood, and positively confronted, the person can be set free and experience profound healing of emotional disorder (see chapter 9).

The Christian Difference

For whatever the reason(s), many people believe that becoming a Christian should make them different regarding their emotions. These people have little difficulty understanding why the unbeliever should experience emotional distress. But as one client said to me, "I thought that when I accepted Christ as Savior, I wouldn't suffer emotionally the way I did before my conversion."

Does being a Christian make any difference in our emotional lives? Do we feel differently because we believe differently? It is clear that before we take up our study of emotional problems we must first understand the basic differences in how believers and unbelievers experience life with their feelings.

First, what is meant by being a Christian? It helps me to define a Christian as a person who has entered into a biblically defined relationship with God, who revealed himself and his plan for our salvation in Christ. Apart from that relationship we are "lost," "separated," "incomplete." In short, our need to be reconciled is our most fundamental need as human beings. Because Adam and Eve sinned in the Garden of Eden, they and the human family that followed were separated from God.

But God had a plan whereby fallen, separated man could once again fellowship with his Creator. To me the Scripture that best summarizes what God did to make this possible is 2 Corinthians 5:19: "God was in Christ, reconciling the world unto himself." And man's response is, in my opinion, most clearly given in Ephesians 2:8: "For by grace are ye saved through faith; and that not of yourselves: it is the gift of God." Therefore, a person becomes a Christian when he or she believes in Christ and what he did by his life, death on the cross, and resurrection to make possible reconciliation with God.

When this reconciliation takes place we experience a profound conversion. My favorite verse on this point is 2 Corinthians 5:17: "If any man be in Christ, he is a new creature: old things are passed away; behold, all things are become new."

Now comes the question, How are we changed? The answer lies in one of Paul's favorite phrases: "in Christ." When we trust Christ as Savior according to the Scriptures, our position radically changes. Before our conversion we are in a self-centered position. The self apart from Christ lacks both insight and power to live in harmony with God, his plan and purpose. But "in Christ" we find God's acceptance and forgiveness, his peace and power—the spiritual resources we need to become all that we are capable of becoming, according to God's will.

Does this mean our emotions will change? Does being "a new creature in Christ Jesus" mean experiencing a basic change in our feelings? The answer from Scripture and recorded human experience is that we are demonstrating wisdom when we speak of Christian ways of understanding, controlling, and expressing our feelings.

How is a Christian supposed to feel? Although the Bible has numerous examples of people describing their feelings, we do not find specific passages telling us how we should feel. Sometimes people refer to verses such as John 15:11 ("These things have I spoken unto you, that my joy might remain in you, and that your joy might be full") to point out that we should feel certain ways. This joy that Jesus brings us is best understood in the light of

a statement by C. S. Lewis: "The opposite of joy is unbe-
lief." This insight helps us to realize that such joy is on a
higher level than our emotions. The joy of which Jesus
spoke accompanies belief in him, thereby freeing joy
from circumstances and conditions which can induce
negative feelings.

The nature of emotions remains the same after conversion. The converted self reacts emotionally to pain, loss,
disappointment, and frustration, as does the uncon-
verted. "But," protests someone, "I thought that as a
Christian I wouldn't hurt as much as I did before my
conversion." Not only is that expectation false, but it also
poorly prepares one for this truth: Sometimes being a
Christian means you will have more pain, not less.

We have only to consider what we, and other Christians, experience when we sin and fail to live up to the
Christian's standard. Being "in Christ" means our relationship to him is the most important thing in life. Whatever disturbs that can cause emotional distress beyond
anything we experienced emotionally as unbelievers.

Any of the countless forms that life's adversities take
cause emotional reaction, whether we are believers or
not. Being "in Christ" does make a difference in our understanding of ourselves, and how we choose to experience our feelings (our attitudes toward them), and how
we direct our behavior. How we feel is important, but
not as important as the meaning we give to our feelings
and how we choose to behave..

Being "in Christ" does not exempt us from failure,
sickness, loss, conflict, pain, and so on. I was not surprised when I came across some research done in this
connection. According to the findings of one study, in an
average local church congregation of five hundred members, at least fifty persons are seriously handicapped by
neurotic conflicts, and at least one hundred by moderate
neurotic symptoms. At least half of the congregation
would complain that their marriages are unhappy and

almost two hundred have been fearful of suffering a nervous breakdown sometime in their lives. About one in every seven has sought professional help for personal or marital problems.

Do such findings mean that Christianity doesn't work? Of course not. Troubled, hurting, confused people are wise when they seek help in local Christian congregations. Without such membership the churches would be empty!

E. Stanley Jones used to tell the story of a little girl who came to church carrying a broken doll in her arms. She found the pastor and tearfully asked, "Is this the place where they mend broken hearts?" Quite a question, isn't it? Is the church the right place for men and women of all ages with various forms of brokenness to come for help? With David we can say with authority, "He heals the brokenhearted" (Ps. 147:3, NIV).

Our Moods and the Rock

In *The Mediator*, Emil Brunner refers to "all these inner moods and feelings as they rise and fall; tossed like the waves of the sea . . . ," emotional experiences with which we are all familiar. But what he adds is a truth that is unique to followers of Christ. These emotions, "like the waves of the sea[,] crash over an immovable sheet of rock, upon which these words are clearly inscribed: I belong to Christ, in spite of everything. In spite of myself, in spite of my moods and feelings, in spite of my experience, of my own importance, even in the sphere of faith. We belong to Christ because of something incomparably more reliable than our human experiences." However the Christian feels, his relationship to his Lord and Savior is eternally based on Christ, his Word, and his work.

According to Scripture, "The just shall live by faith" (Rom. 1:17). Christian faith is the expression of our trust in and reliance on the infallible Word of God. Although faith is deeper than reason or emotion, it does not negate either one. The just person lives by faith that scripturally incorporates reason, emotion, will, and imagination. Our wholeness is not fully achieved until we exercise faith. Christian faith involves the full use of reason, the full expression of emotion, the complete discipline of the will, and the consecration of imagination. Instead of being a weak substitute for those who lack wholeness, Christian faith enlightens, energizes, and directs so that personality is unified, enriched, and expanded.

"The glory of God is man fully alive," wrote Irenaeus, who went on to explain how man becomes "fully alive." "The life of man," he continues, "is the vision of the glory of God." Johann Sebastian Bach wrote thousands of pieces of music. At the bottom of each he wrote *pro gloria Deo* (for the glory of God). His vision of the glory of God sparked his imagination, elevated his thoughts, and energized his efforts. He was living for the ultimate purpose and so became fully alive.

Our Guiding Principles

Serving as the foundation for our study of emotions are the following principles:

1. We experience life in terms of our totality, which means that our emotions are always involved. The value and meaning that we give to the quality of that emotional involvement will vary from one person to another and will change with our personal development.

2. The will, imagination, and emotions are all involved in whatever involves the person. However, research has demonstrated that the imagination is superior to the will in its power to evoke emotional response. For this reason we understand why, when the will and the imagination are battling each other, the imagination invariably wins.

3. Our maturity is partly measured by how well we regulate our emotions. Self-control requires that we man-

age our feelings in ways that increase our sense of well-being, enhance our behavior, and strengthen the quality of our relationships with others. Words such as "positive," "appropriate," and "enhancing" serve as guides for our thinking about self-control.

4. Healthy self-expression is vital to developing a desired sense of health and wholeness. Christianity is more than constraint. Whether we are laughing, loving, crying, worshiping, let it be with all our heart, mind, and soul. As someone has insightfully written, "No virtue is safe that is not enthusiastic; no heart is pure that is not passionate; no life is Christian that is not Christianizing."

This heightened sensitivity to life requires healthy, robust expression of our emotions, which are the very essence of life. Instead of hiding or denying them, we ought to experience them with "the whole of us"!

Unhealthy emotional blockage due to fear, shame, or stuffy sophistication causes all sorts of physical ailments—not to mention personality problems. When my clients—men as well as women—try to hold back the tears, I gently remind them that God gave us those tears for a healthy emotional release. Alfred Tennyson expresses that truth in these lines from *The Princess:*

> Home they brought her warrior dead.
>   She nor swoon'd nor utter'd cry:
> All her maidens, watching, said,
>   "She must weep or she will die."

We are told that when Charles Dickens gave his famous public recitals he became very emotional. When reading about the death of Little Nell or the murder of Nancy, Dickens would drench the stage with his tears. He expressed his understanding of the benefits of weeping in *Oliver Twist:* " 'It opens the lungs, washes the countenance, exercises the eyes and softens down the temper,' said Mr. Bumble. 'So go ahead and cry.' "

Reserve and inhibition have their place, and common sense and maturity help us find it. But whatever hinders openness and spontaneity should not be associated with any desirable pattern of development. Poise should include passion and stability should include spontaneity! A person should grow away from rigidity and fearful inhibition toward the ability to say yes, no, and whoopee! I'll always remember the morning that my father, my second son, David, and I were getting ready to go fishing. We were eagerly wolfing down breakfast when someone said, "This is the day which the LORD hath made; we will rejoice and be glad in it" (Ps. 118:24). David, who was about nine or ten years old at the time, decided to give his version in the style and spirit of a buccaneer: "This is the day that the Lord hath made—Ya ho! Ya ho! Ya ho!" And that celebrative attitude toward life is Christian to the core.

One who exemplified this rare ability to live each moment to the fullest, whether it be sweet or bitter, was Katherine Mansfield. Although tuberculosis was slowly taking her life, she sent her husband explicit instructions for making strawberry jam. She told him how many berries, how much sugar, and then exclaimed: "God! as I write I freeze, I burn, I desire, with a passion that is pain, to be these all in my little bib and tucker." After she died at thirty-four years of age, her husband wrote, "She suffered greatly, she delighted greatly. But her suffering and her delight were never partial, they filled the whole of her."

Now that kind of behavior is not only refreshing but also uniquely Christian. Study the life of Christ as we are given it by his biographers—Matthew, Mark, Luke, and John. They observed a remarkable variety of emotional behaviors, showing that in this respect as well as others, Christ was fashioned as a man (Phil. 2:8). Jesus wept (John 11:35), sorrowed (Matt. 26:37), felt hunger (Luke 4:2), was weary (John 4:6), became angry (Mark 3:5), experienced agony (Luke 22:44), and felt forsaken by God (Matt. 27:46). We do not witness this until we read about the crucifixion, when Christ spoke with a loud voice: "My God, my God, why hast thou forsaken me?" (Matt. 27:46).

Passing from physical pain to the indescribable agony of mind and spirit, Christ identified with sinful humanity and experienced the separating effects of sin. The rejection that he felt wrenched from his soul a cry that expresses the sentiments of every human heart separated from God. He experienced the abandonment, the loneliness of souls suffering from "that forsaken feeling." Whether it is recognized or not, this sense of being without God is the greatest cause of mental agony in human experience. Because the cure is spiritual, it lies beyond the abilities of psychiatrists and psychologists who lack spiritual insight.

5. Negative feelings should not be allowed to convey their reality as the truth. Feelings of worthlessness, rejection, hopelessness, or helplessness can be painfully real, but must be evaluated in reference to sacred Scripture.

6. Positive feelings should not be allowed to convey their reality as the truth. The lines of a popular contemporary song state, "It can't be wrong when it feels so right." However, Scripture, as well as tested experience, exposes the fallacy of allowing emotion to act as a reliable guide to right and wrong.

7. The principle used to unify our study of the emotions is that we are made up of body, mind, and spirit. Each of these aspects of the person acts on and is acted on by the other two. How we feel is affected by how we think and how we think is affected by how we feel. How we think is affected by our philosophy of life, our values—our heart, the center of the self. When the nature of the whole man is thus conceptualized, we are led to give importance to all those factors and forces within and without the person that enhance life. For the body

this would include nutrition, rest, exercise, sexual expression (within biblical limits); for the mind, truth, hope, belief, a sense of significance, of being loved and of loving, of having a place in life's total scheme, of serving a purpose satisfying to ourselves and useful to others; for the spirit, a personal, meaningful, growing relationship with God who was in Christ reconciling each of us to himself.

Because the emotions can never be divorced from the person, they are involved in everything that affects the person.

The Heart of the Problem

Actually the heart of the problem is the problem of the heart. In biblical literature the term *heart* denotes the center and focus of the rational, emotional, and intentional dimensions of the person. In modern psychological terminology, we would refer to these dimensions as cognitive, affective, and volitional. The deepest truth about us can be found at the heart's level, for there reside our motives, values, aspirations, moral leanings, what and whom we reverence. It was his profound understanding of this that caused King Solomon, the wisest man of his day, to admonish, "Keep thy heart with all diligence, for out of it are the issues of life" (Prov. 4:23). James Moffat translates it,

> Guard above all things, guard your inner self,
>   for so you live and prosper.

Solomon's insights into the inner man can be found in the Book of Proverbs. In *Baker's Dictionary of Theology* this helpful summary is given: "The heart is the seat of wisdom (2:10); of trust (or confidence) (3:5); diligence (4:23); perverseness (6:14); wicked imagination (6:18); lust (6:25); subtlety (7:10); understanding (8:5); deceit (12:20);

folly (12:23); heaviness (12:25); bitterness (14:10); sorrow (14:13); backsliding (14:14); cheerfulness (15:13); knowledge (15:14); joy (15:30); pride (16:5); haughtiness (18:12); prudence (18:15); fretfulness (19:3); envy (23:17)."

Such knowledge allows us to have a greater appreciation for the insight shared by Jeremiah, one of the major prophets in the Old Testament.

> Deep is a man's mind, deeper than all else,
>   on evil bent;
>   who can fathom it?
> "I the Eternal search the mind,
>   I test the heart . . ." (17:9–10, *Moffat*).

This brings us in our study of negative emotions to the place of true understanding. How we feel, think, and direct our lives comes from our innermost self, the heart. For this reason we demonstrate wisdom when we become students of sacred Scripture. It is in God's Word, not in the secular writings of philosophers and behavioral scientists, that we find divinely revealed truth about ourselves. "For the Word that God speaks is alive and active: it cuts more keenly than any two-edged sword: it strikes through to the place where soul and spirit meet, to the innermost intimacies of a man's being: it exposes the very thoughts and motives of a man's heart" (Heb. 4:12, *Phillips*).

Only the word of God has the power to illumine, cleanse, and renew our hearts. Here then is our guiding principle as we begin our study of finding positive ways of handling our negative emotions. Our emotional selves are best understood in relationship to the heart. When our hearts belong to Christ, and are enlightened, cleansed, and renewed by careful study of sacred Scripture, then we can understand and positively manage the negative emotions that we all experience in this earthly pilgrimage.

So we come to the place of understanding when we realize that more important than the emotions a person has is the person having the emotion. Is that person in the right position—in Christ? If so, that is the place of understanding. In that precious position, whatever emotion the person has, that emotion can be victoriously managed by the person!

2

Handling Guilt Wisely

Recently someone asked me, "What problem do most of your clients need help with?"

I thought of the kinds of problems that are most frequently brought to my consulting room—fear, hatred, feelings of inferiority, loss of meaning in one's life, frustration, and guilt. Of these I would say that guilt is the most common problem. In spite of modern man's determination to deny the reality of guilt and to explain it away, we are discovering that the burden of guilt is not relieved simply by calling it something else.

We must understand guilt before we can help a person who is experiencing guilt. For people can be helped to experience something more valuable than a mere negating of guilt feelings. People can be shown how to deal *creatively* with their guilt. For, when guilt is properly understood and acted on, it can be a great influence for living *more* fully, *more* productively, *more* joyfully. Thus guilt can promote our development, making us "more than we are."

The critical question facing us as we begin our study is, What is the most reliable source for a proper understanding of our subject? As Solomon noted, "A man of sense defers to authority" (Prov. 10:8, *Moffatt*). My training at the university exposed me to many "authorities." My professors identified the leading thinkers and explained their theories. While I appreciate what I learned from my formal training, I am convinced, after more than twenty-five years of counseling experience, that the most reliable authority for guiding, explaining, and promoting life is the Bible. In the sacred Scriptures we find the most dependable insights into such questions as, What is guilt? Where does it come from? What are its effects? How can it be treated?

The Nature of Guilt

In seeking to understand the nature of guilt, it may be helpful to classify the two kinds of guilt: (1) guilt as a *moral condition*, and (2) guilt as a *personality disturbance*.

First, regarding our moral condition, the Bible tells us that "there is none righteous, no, not one" (Rom. 3:10). That is, we have fallen short of God's standard of living, his moral law. Because of sin we are separated—alienated—from our Creator. We are guilty because we have violated God's moral law and because we are alienated from him.

Second, a personality disturbance due to a sense of guilt goes beyond our moral condition to moral awareness. This has its origin in our conscience. According to the Bible, this moral awareness goes all the way back to the beginning of human history. Because Adam and Eve were morally aware of their disobedience to God, they experienced what we call a guilty conscience—they hid from God's presence (Gen. 3:8). Although the word *conscience* does not appear in the Old Testament, the concept is present and is expressed by the word *heart*. This Old Testament term is very appropriate, for there is no heartache like a guilty conscience. After David committed adultery with Bathsheba his heart "smote him" (2 Sam. 24:10). He describes his bitter anguish in Psalm 32:1–5 and 51:1–9.

Conscience

Scripture teaches us that conscience is inborn (innate, inherited) and universal: "For when the Gentiles, which have not the law, do by nature the things contained in the law, these . . . shew the work of the law written in their hearts, their conscience also bearing witness, and their thoughts the meanwhile accusing or else excusing one another . . ." (Rom. 2:14–15). Although conscience may be influenced by environment, education, habit, or training, it is not the *result* of any of these factors.

Our conscience functions in three ways. First, it urges us to do what we know is right and restrains us from doing what we know is wrong. Second, it acts as the standard by which we make our moral evaluation. Third, it passes judgment on our own actions, expressing itself in our personality. Wrong motives, choices, and deeds result in inner disturbance—shame, distress, remorse. Right behavior brings its own reward of conscience—inner peace, and a sense of divine, social, and personal approval.

We can identify a number of well-known descriptions of conscience. First there is the *erring conscience*, which is not an accurate expression. Conscience does not err. Error is caused by faulty learning and standards accepted and acted on by the mind. Next, there is the *narrow, morbid*, or *perverted conscience*. These adjectives describe a conscience that has lost its health and balance. Again this language is misleading, for a conscience does not simply *become* perverted unless a person perverts it. Further, there is the *dulled, calloused*, or *dead conscience*. The most dangerous of all moral states, the dulled conscience is the result of repeated willful, conscious wrongdoing. Moral insensitivity is the terrible consequence of deliberate refusal over a long period of time to heed the voice of right conduct. Finally, there is the *good, healthy, sound conscience*. When behavior conforms to beliefs which are based on a growing understanding of scriptural principles, then we possess a good conscience.

Conscience is the inward sense of right and wrong. It is the awareness that we should do right; but it cannot be completely relied on to tell us what is right. The reason for this is that our understanding of what is right and wrong is influenced by so many factors. It begins with what we learn from our parents, and includes what we learn from our relatives, teachers, ministers, friends, books, the mass media, and so forth. None of these sources is infallible; thus our knowledge of right and wrong can be faulty.

What is right must be determined by reliable authority. This is critical to mental health. It is important to remember that conscience is our moral monitor; it admonishes us to do what *we* think is right. We must be careful not to give conscience the same authority as we give Scriptures.

Sin

At this point we must understand the meaning of sin, because the ideas of guilt and conscience make sense only with respect to sin. The biblical definition of sin has three aspects. First, sin is wrongdoing. "Sin is the transgression of the law" (1 John 3:4b). Sin is moral failure, disobedience to the divine will. Second, sin is failing to do right. "To him that knoweth to do good, and doeth it not, to him it is sin" (James 4:17). Such sins are known as "sins of omission," that is, purposely avoiding what we know we should do. Third, "whatsoever is not of faith is sin" (Rom. 14:23). If we cannot believe that a certain course of action is in harmony with the will of God, then it is sinful for us to follow that course of action, even if the action in itself is legitimate. To go against this personal conviction is to act "not [according to] faith," thus to sin. Our definition of sin therefore includes transgression, neglect, and faithless action regarding God's will.

Unfortunately, it is no longer fashionable to take sin seriously. When people do refer to their sins, they usually do it with self-indulgent humor rather than a sense of shame. Their acknowledgment implies, "Oh, well, I guess I'm just human like everybody else." Worse yet is the hypocritically pious attitude that ignores sin entirely: "I thank God I'm not as other men are."

Well, then, what *is* so bad about sin? We more clearly understand the horror of sin when we realize that it is "against" God, others, and even ourselves. Sin is involved when someone has been hurt, offended, mistreated. All sin has elements of willful defiance, rebellion, disloyalty.

Most of the attention given to sin focuses on wrongs intended and/or committed socially. But seldom do we realize that we can sin against *ourselves*. Consider the observation made by William James:

> Most of us feel as if we live habitually with a sort of cloud weighing on us, below our highest notch of clearness in discernment, sureness in reasoning, or firmness in deciding. Compared with what we ought to be, we are only half awake. Our fires are dampened, our drafts are checked, we are making use of only a small part of our possible mental and physical resources.

This sense of what we ought to be but are not is one of the greatest reasons why many of us have guilt feelings.

All sin is, first of all, against God. To know this is to have a "God-consciousness" that motivates us to live in harmony with God's will. When Joseph was tempted by Potiphar's wife, his reason for abstaining from sexual immorality was expressed this way: "How then can I do this great wickedness, and sin against God?" (Gen. 39:9).

To lose our consciousness of God has fearful consequences. In his letter to the church in Rome, Paul writes,

> Since they did not think it worthwhile to retain the knowledge of God, he gave them over to a depraved mind, to do what ought not to be done. They have become filled with every kind of wickedness, evil, greed and depravity. They are full of envy, murder, strife, de-

ceit and malice. They are gossips, slanderers, God-haters, insolent, arrogant and boastful; they invent ways of doing evil; they disobey their parents, they are senseless, faithless, heartless, ruthless. Although they know God's righteous decree that those who do such things deserve death, they not only continue to do these very things, but also approve of those who practice them (Rom. 1:28–32, NIV).

In spite of sin's effects, there is no man who does not sin: "If we say we have no sin, we deceive ourselves, and the truth is not in us" (1 John 1:8). Some acts of sin are, however, more deliberate than others, and we must understand the importance of *motive*. For example, carelessly exceeding the speed limit is very different from deliberately running a red light. Likewise, to slip unintentionally into a sin is vastly different from willful, deliberate disobedience to the known will of God.

Since sin is disobedience to God it would seem that the more we sin, the more aware of it we would become. Unfortunately the reverse is true. The more sin is repeated, the *less* we are aware of it. As sin increases in our experience, our knowledge of it decreases. Sin cannot understand holiness (purity of heart); but holiness understands sin. The eyes of the heart are sharpened or dulled according to the extent we live in harmony with God's will. And moral perception has value beyond our comprehension.

The Voice of a Disturbed Conscience

When we sin, the conscience becomes disturbed. Our moral monitor becomes aware of a moral truth. And one of the great characteristics of truth is that it seeks to make itself known—"Be sure your sin will find you out" (Num. 32:23). But this sort of truth—knowledge of one's own deceit, immorality, cruelty, and the like—is very painful to admit to oneself, to others, even to God. Our need to preserve our own sense of worth is so great that when we are guilty of wrongdoing we very often attempt to conceal it, instead of dealing with it honestly, openly, and creatively (i.e., biblically).

But conscience has a voice that will not be silenced. As Shakespeare has one of his characters exclaim, "My conscience hath a thousand tongues . . . ." Nothing—not even medicine, psychoanalysis, alcohol, drugs, sleep, travel, or diversions—can put an offended conscience to rest until the person deals with it scripturally.

The effects of a disturbed conscience have been experienced by all of us. We understand Huck Finn when he said, "Conscience takes up more room than all the rest of a person's insides." A troubled conscience can speak its disturbing truth in an amazing variety of ways, expressing itself in various physical and psychological symptoms. Dr. O. Hobart Mowrer, former president of the American Psychological Association, has classified guilt symptoms in two ways. Type I symptoms are those that the autonomic nervous system produces involuntarily (that is, physical reactions over which a person has no control). Type II symptoms are those that are self-defeating reactions to the Type I symptoms.

In addition to Dr. Mowrer's list, we must add such symptoms as a sense of being separated from God, a fear of God's wrath, the inability to pray effectively, and a loss of desire to read the Scriptures and to attend public worship. All these symptoms belong to the spiritual dimension of personality as it relates to God.

Symptoms, Type I	*Symptoms, Type II*
tension	withdrawal
anxiety	escapism
depression	invalidism
self-hate	fantasy

fear of death	grandiosity
panic	suicide
loss of appetite	rationalization
accident proneness	resentment
work inhibition	blaming others
poor memory	attacking others
tics, stuttering	self-pity
insomnia	reassurance
fatigue	compulsions
sleepiness	rituals
irritability	busyness
self-doubt	overeating
indecision	abuse of sex
loneliness	intoxicants
nightmares	narcotics
sense of unreality	tranquilizers
obsessions	
hypochondria	
hysteria	
hallucinations	
delusions	

Nowhere do we find the effects of a guilty conscience described more movingly than in the Psalms. After committing adultery with Bathsheba, David discovered that being Israel's king did not exempt him from the judgment of his own conscience. In Psalm 51:1–12 he expresses his guilt and sorrow:

Have mercy upon me, O God, according to thy lovingkindness: according unto the multitude of thy tender mercies blot out my transgressions. Wash me thoroughly from mine iniquity, and cleanse me from my sin. For I acknowledge my transgressions: and my sin is ever before me. Against thee, thee only, have I sinned, and done this evil in thy sight: that thou mightest be justified when thou speakest, and be clear when thou judgest. Behold, I was shapen in iniquity; and in sin did my mother conceive me. Behold, thou desirest truth in the inward parts: and in the hidden part thou shalt make me to know wisdom. Purge me with hyssop, and I shall be clean: wash me, and I shall be whiter than snow. Make me to hear joy and gladness; that the bones which thou hast broken may rejoice. Hide thy face from my sins, and blot out all mine iniquities. Create in me a clean heart, O God; and renew a right spirit within me. Cast me not away from thy presence; and take not thy holy spirit from me. Restore unto me the joy of thy salvation; and uphold me with thy free spirit.

A careful study of David's description of his guilt reveals intense spiritual suffering and a sense of being alienated from God. There is no ache like that of the heart that has lost a sense of divine presence. Once a person experiences a personal relationship to God (who revealed himself in Christ) that relationship becomes life's highest value.

Often a sense of sin is accompanied by expecting God to "get even." Such was the case of a wife who came to me for counseling; she said she was leaving her husband. Their marital conflict at first appeared to be over whether or not to have a child. She did not want one and finally she was able to confess the reason. Prior to her marriage she had an affair with a married man, became pregnant, and had an abortion. Later she gave her life to Christ, and met the fine Christian man whom she married. "But I feel so guilty about my past," she tearfully explained. "I'm so afraid that if I have a child, God will punish me for what I did by allowing something bad to happen to my baby." No wonder she did not want to have a child! Like so many others, she was suffering unnecessarily from a guilt complex. She was tormented by the haunting thought, "You have committed a horrible wrong. You must pay. And since you destroyed your baby conceived in sin, you will atone by either losing your baby or giving birth to a baby that will be handicapped."

Although the relationship between moral health and mental health is clearly established, we must not blame all mental disturbances on a sense of sin. An enlightened point of view would certainly include a recognition of *physical* causes such as organic changes in the brain, glandular disturbances, and abnormalities in the central nervous system. What is dangerous, however, is the all-too-common practice of attempting to explain away a sense of guilt that *has* been caused by sin. Such attempts lead to a worsening of the disturbance as time goes on.

"But," some would protest, "having a sense of sin leads to a morbid frame of mind or a guilt complex." Not so. There is no evidence to support such an argument, and to refuse to acknowledge sin when it *is* present is to cut off any chance for cure. To recognize sin is our basis for hope, for the gift of forgiveness can be received only when we realize our need for it. Actually, any person who can accept the responsibility for sinning has hope for a better future. Blaming human nature (biological urges, instincts, etc.) or our environment (parents, poverty, etc.) leads to despair. If we are able to say, "I'm to blame for this," we can identify the problem so that it has a solution, possibilities. To put the blame on whatever or whomever cannot be changed leads to feelings of futility, hopelessness, and a sense of being imprisoned by life. To be able to blame ourselves means to accept the responsibility for our choices. If we *are* free to choose our way into our future, we can begin *now* to make life better.

The Problem of Self-Honesty

One of the most difficult problems we face is admitting we have done wrong. Each of us develops, with the passing of the years, a sense of rightness about his pattern of living. Solomon expressed it this way: "Every way of a man is right in his own eyes" (Prov. 21:2). We human beings defend ourselves against whatever and whomever would disprove this cherished sense of rightness. Our values, beliefs, and attitudes define us to ourselves. And this definition of self is protected at all costs, as if to learn that being wrong, weak, or sinful would mean loss of this self we regard so highly.

But observe what can happen when we sin, make a mistake, show weakness—anything that can cause the conscience to generate a sense of guilt. We begin to rationalize, to justify ourselves. A person may say, "Okay, so I told a fib, but at least I did not clobber him which is what I really wanted to do." Or, "I guess I am guilty of resentment, but that's not as bad as what he feels toward me."

Let us name this most unsavory human characteristic—*pride*. How it resists change and how it masquerades to avoid recognition! To be able to accept blame from ourselves and others is remarkably rare. And sometimes behind the confession "I'm willing to accept the blame" is the same unhealthy pride strutting in its "courage and honesty."

> Admitting my pride was a long time coming
> Self-honesty is an easy ball to fumble
> But I've been making such great progress—
> Now I'm proud because I'm humble!
> —Louis O. Caldwell

What is most frustrating of all is the sad truth that a person infected with pride has no idea of his infection. At all costs such a person keeps from himself the horrible truth of its presence. And the strategy whereby this recognition is resisted is called *hypocrisy*.

One of its most subtle strategies is to cling to a sense of

guilt, for it is far more difficult to change than to feel guilty. Continuing a wrong pattern of believing and behaving can be atoned for by feeling guilty, and the sense of guilt may be needed if the person does not want to change his behavior. The logic goes like this: "I'm doing wrong, but I'm paying for it." Other disguises for pride are a showy humility, false modesty, supersensitivity, fear of trying, difficulty in accepting compliments, bemoaning inadequacies, contempt for others, perpetual giving, do-goodism, perfectionism, and so on.

No one is as blind as the person who will not admit that he cannot see. Often he cannot see that he is in greater need of seeing than are those whom *he* thinks are blind. He is like the Pharisee in Jesus' parable in Luke 18:10–14:

> Two men went up into the temple to pray; the one a Pharisee, and the other a publican. The Pharisee stood and prayed thus with himself, God, I thank thee, that I am not as other men are, extortioners, unjust, adulterers, or even as this publican. I fast twice in the week, I give tithes of all that I possess. And the publican, standing afar off, would not lift up so much as his eyes unto heaven, but smote upon his breast, saying, God be merciful to me a sinner. I tell you, this man went down to his house justified rather than the other: for every one that exalteth himself shall be abased; and he that humbleth himself shall be exalted.

A modern psychological paraphrase of the Pharisee's prayer could go something like this: "I thank thee, O God (if you exist and are not just a projection of my earthly father), that I have been advised by my therapist that it is old-fashioned to feel guilty and that sin exists only for the ignorant and those who take religion too seriously. There could, I admit, be something wrong with me—but other people are so much worse than I am that whatever could be wrong with me is not really that bad. Take that publican, for example. I'll bet he doesn't even fast or give to any charitable organizations, as I do. In fact, the more I think about it, the less I feel the need to pray."

The second form of self-deception is denial. Ignoring or denying the voice of a striken conscience might remove its voice from consciousness, but not from the personality. The act of deliberately removing from the conscious mind anything that the person is unwilling to acknowledge is called repression and is extremely harmful to the personality. Few writers have communicated this as memorably as Shakespeare in *Macbeth*. After conspiring to murder the king, Lady Macbeth is unable to sleep soundly and compulsively continues to wash her hands. Finally, the burden of guilt accompanied by concealment of her terrible secret causes her to "break down." When the physician visits her, Macbeth makes this plea:

> Canst thou not minister to a mind diseas'd,
> Pluck from the memory a rooted sorrow,
> Raze out the written troubles of the brain,
> And with some sweet oblivious antidote
> Cleanse the stuff'd bosom of that perilous stuff
> Which weighs upon the heart?

Physical problems are frequently the result of repression of an outraged conscience. It is interesting to note that the body can bear pain better than the mind can. Because this is true there can be a transference of spiritual and psychological distress to the body. It is as if the nonphysical part of the person says to the body, "Here, I can't take any more of this burden. You take it." Thus what began as a spiritual-psychological problem becomes also a physical problem. Sooner or later the body tells the truth about the person's inner world. Because of the unity of personality, what affects one dimension affects the whole person in some way.

This discovery has caused the word *psychosomatic* to

take a prominent place in the vocabulary dealing with physical problems. It comes from the Greek words *psyche,* meaning "mind" or "soul," and *soma,* meaning "body." Psychosomatic illnesses are physical problems having a nonorganic cause.

Among the most difficult cases are those people who have repressed their guilt and defended themselves against its recognition by efforts that are "religious" or "spiritual." Guilt is often lurking behind the kind of conscientiousness over trivial matters that overlooks the more important issues of love, justice, mercy, and truth. This was the problem of the Pharisees who were rebuked by Christ for straining at a gnat and swallowing a camel (Matt. 23:24). Without realizing why, these people became arrogant, intolerant, and unforgiving.

An example of "masking guilt" was a college student who once said to me, "I have trouble relating to people, especially Christians. They seem to be so much better than I am." As the counseling session continued, she began to confess several sexual sins in her past which she feared her Christian friends might find out about. "What would they think of me if they knew?" she worried. This college student followed the familiar pattern of sin→guilt→concealment—but dealt with it in her mind in such a way that she told herself, "My problem is that other Christians are better than I am."

Repression helps to explain why a person feels guilty and does not know the reason. Such persons often describe feelings of self-hate, depression, inferiority, loneliness, torment. These painful feelings are made worse when one does not know their cause. To get relief from this, a person may resort to extreme measures to attach feelings of guilt to a cause—any cause, no matter how wrong it may be.

Another way of mishandling an offended conscience is to substitute a socially acceptable reason for the real one. Jesus once said of a certain man, "But he desir[ed] to justify himself . . ." (Luke 10:29). Jesus was describing what all of us do.

One of the most common methods of dealing with our guilt is to refuse to acknowledge it in ourselves and to project it onto others. As someone has aptly stated:

> Let each man learn to know himself,
>   To gain that knowledge let him labor,
> Correct those failings in himself,
>   Which he condemns so in his neighbor.

Finally, it is helpful to understand guilt feelings that are due to growth.* Many people suffer guilt reactions during a period of change. Change is often accompanied by anxiety and a sense of wrongness. Great inner conflict can be experienced, for part of the self resists the change and part desires it. If the change really does mean growth, the person must recognize it and give whole-hearted consent, if personality health is to be maintained.

In this connection it is helpful to learn to distinguish between reactions *to* people, things, ideas, feelings, and responses *against*. Reactions *to* are purely emotional, whereas responses *against* are intentional. The first response is simply to be experienced and controlled; the second is to be morally evaluated. And that is why guilt should only be associated with responses *against* and never with reactions *to*.

This can be illustrated by the case of Jason (not his real name). As he talked about the mistreatment he had received from some relatives, his anger and hurt—reactions *to* mistreatment—became very evident. "Is it wrong for me to feel this way?" he asked. Added to these feelings of confusion was the fact that he had not shared this burden with anyone, not even his wife. The

---

*Growth is defined as change in a Christ-approved direction. This means that change is in harmony not only with biblical concepts and principles but also with the Spirit of Christ.

guilt and stress related to secrecy were tormenting him, driving his blood pressure dangerously high and robbing him of appetite and sleep. In addition to learning the difference between reactions *to* and responses *against*, the client was encouraged to share his burden with his wife. In a few days he had completely regained his peace of mind, accompanied by normal blood pressure, appetite, and sleep.

There is no disturbance like that of an enraged conscience unleashing its condemnation. No matter how carefully the self-defense system has been developed, it cannot prevent the sense of guilt from breaking through. During the conscious waking hours the torment can come in the form of painful regret, remorse, depression, inappropriate or compulsive behavior such as frequent washing of hands and overreacting to people and problems. Nor does sleep necessarily quiet the mishandled conscience. For the guilty conscience can discharge frightening dreams and nightmares into the mind.

The Biblical Solution

The creative way to deal with guilt resulting from sin is given us in the Scriptures. We are called upon to *repent*. John, the forerunner of Christ, brought this message, "Repent ye: for the kingdom of heaven is at hand" (Matt. 3:2). Later, Jesus himself declared, "I came not to call the righteous, but sinners to repentance" (Mark 2:17).

There is abundant evidence that most people do not have a clear understanding of this important word. Repentance is a process which has four parts: confession, contrition, reparation, and change or amendment. If this seems unnecessarily complicated, consider the example of a marital conflict. A husband and wife are arguing. One of them makes an unfair accusation and the friendly relationship between them is suddenly ruptured. Suppose the guilty one wants to make up—or in biblical terms, has the desire to repent. To restore the relationship, the guilty person must admit he was wrong, that what was said was unfair or untrue. This is *confession*. This must be followed by an expression of regret, "I'm sorry, honey, for hurting you with that statement." This is *contrition*. After this, steps should be taken to restore the relationship, such as reaching out to the offended mate and saying, "Please forgive me, I love you and do not want to hurt you." This is making *reparation*. And then it is necessary to show by a change in future behavior that the desire to repent was truly sincere. This is *amendment*. If any of the four parts is missing, the repentance process is incomplete and the relationship is not restored.

Likewise when we turn to God in repentance we must be sure that it is complete. We start with confession. "He that covereth his sins shall not prosper: but whoso confesseth and forsaketh them shall have mercy" (Prov. 28:13). The only sins God will not forgive are those we refuse to confess. "If we confess our sins, he is faithful and just to forgive us our sins, and to cleanse us from all unrighteousness" (I John 1:9). What power to lift the burden of guilt do such words have! It is profoundly therapeutic to know our sin will be remembered no more (Jer. 31:34). Our sin is removed from us "as far as the east is from the west" (Ps. 103:12); it is behind God's back (Isa. 38:17).

Since all sin is against God, confession of sin should be made to God. But confession does not stop with God. If we have sinned against another person, confession must be made to him. In James's epistle we are told, "Confess your faults one to another . . . that ye may be healed" (5:16).

But repentance goes beyond confessing evil deeds to confessing evil *purposes*. Simon, the magician, was urged by Peter to "repent therefore of this thy wickedness, and pray God, if perhaps the thought of thine heart may be forgiven thee" (Acts 8:22). This reminds us that *inside* the person is where sin should be dealt with. It is the wrong intent, motive, purpose, desire—the unobserved wickedness—for which repentance is the hardest to make. For example, if a person slanders another person, he can say, "I made a mistake, I said the wrong thing—I'm sorry." This kind of repentance does not involve the total person as much as when he admits, "My motive was wrong. I intended to hurt you. I'm sorry." *That* kind of acknowledgment hurts, because a person is more closely linked with his motives than with his behavior. But genuine repentance includes repentance of our wrong motives—"the thought of [our] heart"—which have opposed the purpose of God.

Admittedly, this lays bare the soul and generates fear and shame. But when the wounds of the heart are exposed to the Healer, he gently and thoroughly heals them, restoring the suffering person to wholeness. In dealing biblically with our guilt, it is vital, then, to have the companionship of Christ. In his company our best desires are expressed, and our worst is honestly acknowledged and dealt with so as to please him. For in walking with him we learned the truth of his words: "I have come that they might have life, and that they might have it more abundantly" (John 10:10).

Sometimes confession is regarded as a way of atonement for sin. Part of the value of confessing sin (or admitting a sense of wrongdoing) lies in externalizing it, so that the mind can deal with it reasonably. As long as the problem remains internal, inside the self, it links itself with other ideas, experiences, or feelings. This makes a clear understanding of what the problem is and how best to handle it very difficult, perhaps impossible. Getting the problem outside the self (externalizing it) isolates it and makes it possible to be understood and creatively managed. By externalizing through confession, the conscience will not be checked by reliable authority, by reasonably relating to Scripture. This has two major advantages: (1) the conscience will not be ruled by exterior codes and prohibitions lacking proper authority, and (2) the conscience will not be ruled by interior references—feelings, impulses, hunches, imaginings, and such. Frequently I have witnessed the results of what William James calls "exteriorising our rottenness" through confession. This action has remarkable power to unburden the guilt-ridden conscience.

But who should we choose to hear our confession? The utmost caution should be used in making this decision. Qualities to look for would be integrity, spiritual insight, and maturity. With these qualifications would come the ability to keep a confidence, as well as to give understanding and scriptural guidance. More than a listener's sympathy is required if the burden of guilt is to be removed so that confession leads to a more creative life.

Guilty people all too frequently have their guilt poorly understood and treated. Outside the church in consulting rooms they have their guilt either explained away or ridiculed. Inside the church they have their guilt handled all too often in the same way; but what is worse, they are likely to receive judgment or censorship. As one widely-traveled minister recently said to me, "It is hard for most people to believe that another person can listen to confessions of sin, ignorance, carelessness, and the like, without condemning." And it is for this reason, perhaps more than any other, that a guilt-ridden person fears revealing himself to another Christian. Instead of denouncing and moralizing we should be understanding and assisting those with intolerable burdens of guilt. Wise was he who said, "Never take your wounds to anybody but a healer."

Lacking these insights, many people have made the mistake of confessing to a mate, for example, and discovering that the confession was too burdensome to handle. My files contain tragic evidence of how unwise confessions can shatter relationships and ruin lives. It should be added, however, that in some cases, confession to a mate saves the marriage. This can happen if, after hearing the confession, the person sinned against can use it as an opportunity to strengthen the relationship. This is done by forgiveness, understanding the cause of the problem, and determination to correct the problem.

When trying to determine the wisdom of confessing a serious misdeed to a mate, child, or parent, it is wise to seek the guidance of someone properly qualified in this kind of problem, such as a Christian therapist.

Before confession is made, the following questions should be carefully considered:

1. What do I need to confess?
2. Why do I need to confess?
3. Who should hear this confession?
4. How should I confess?

After confessing their sins, however, a great many people continue feeling guilty. Often this is due to the effects of sin. "I thought that after I confessed my sins that everything would be all right," is what many people say. These people need to understand that when we are forgiven our relationship to God is restored. The restoration of this relationship does *not* cancel out the consequences of our wrongdoing. "Be not deceived; God is not mocked: for whatsoever a man soweth, that shall he also reap" (Gal. 6:7).

Frequently clients say, "I believe that God has forgiven me; if only I could forgive myself." This is usually followed by descriptions of disbelief over the wrong that was done. "I can't believe that I did that," or "I never thought I was capable of such a thing," are common statements. It is painful to realize "I am the kind of person capable of stealing, or lying, or commiting adultery." Such exposure of character flaws can cause guilt feelings to linger.

The greatest reason for the soul's distress is not sin, guilt, or feelings of guilt, but rather separation from God. Until or unless the separation problem is solved we suffer from a sense of cosmic loneliness and incompleteness compared to which all our other problems are secondary. Confession of sin, repentance of sin, and appropriate reparation are the biblically-defined ways of restoring our relationship with God. Obeying biblical authority enables us not only to be in the right relationship with God, but also to learn creative uses of guilt and guilt feelings in our relationships with others.

Conscience is functioning as it should when it compels us to examine ourselves honestly and accurately. As Dr. Carl Jung wrote, "Conscience, and particularly a bad conscience, can be a gift from heaven, a genuine grace, if used as a superior self-criticism." By creatively using a guilty conscience, we not only can grow toward God, we can develop richer relationships with others. And, we will discover as a by-product that the inner world of our personality is unified and healed.

True repentance is always accompanied by godly sorrow (contrition). "Godly sorrow brings repentance that leads to salvation and leaves no regret, but worldly sorrow brings death" (2 Cor. 7:10, NIV). Some sorrow takes the form of morbid remorse and obsessive regret over what has been done. Some are sorry merely because they were caught in a sin. Such sorrow is not contrition, but self-centered sentimentalism. True contrition is a deep sense of sorrow for an offense against the God who loves us. As David wrote, "The Lord is nigh unto them that are of a broken heart" (Ps. 34:18).

Many people burdened with the consequences of wrongdoing go to a counselor hoping to get some relief. Any relief that they experience is only temporary, however, unless their sorrow leads them to turn from their wrongdoing. This is the kind of repentance which soundness of mind and heart requires. The ability to identify the wrong is the first step. The next step is to turn from it in true, sincere repentance. This is the biblical way to unburden the personality and to bring the joy that accompanies a right relationship to God.

In Matthew 5, Jesus clearly teaches that *reparation* must be added to confession and contrition. After we confess our sin against God in genuine sorrow, we must do what is necessary to correct our relationships with others. Jesus said, "If thou bring thy gift to the altar, and there rememberest that thy brother hath ought against thee; leave there thy gift before the altar, and go thy way; first be reconciled to thy brother, and then come and offer thy gift" (Matt. 5:23–24).

In the next chapter, Christ said, "For if ye forgive men their trespasses, your heavenly Father will also forgive you: but if ye forgive not men their trespasses, neither will your Father forgive your trespasses" (Matt. 6:14–15). These two statements clearly teach the necessity of assuming our responsibility for our interpersonal relationships. Any unwillingness on our part to put matters right with our fellow man acts as a barrier to receiving God's forgiveness. It also prevents the conscience from being at rest. This clear teaching of God is not easily obeyed, for as a client recently admitted, "Asking God for forgiveness is a lot easier than asking my wife."

Yet the willingness to make reparation is the sure evidence that we are adequately dealing with the causes of the disturbed conscience. When Zacchaeus, the wealthy publican, met Christ and "received him joyfully" the change from his former behavior (dishonest business practices) was dramatic. We are given this remarkable record: "And Zacchaeus stood, and said unto the Lord; Behold, Lord, the half of my goods I give to the poor; and if I have taken any thing from any man by false accusation, I restore him fourfold." When Jesus heard this, he said, "This day is salvation come to this house" (see Luke 19:1–10).

By making reparation we, in John Wesley's phrase, "put the fire out of our bosom." A memorable example of this was an attractive, intelligent Christian in her thirties who suffered from colitis and numerous other physical problems. She had herself admitted to the hospital and underwent a thorough physical examination. The results showed that her illness had no physical cause. So, she came to my office. The counseling sessions revealed a number of interpersonal relationship problems, unpaid bills, and the like. She was able to understand the need to correct the interpersonal conflicts and to assure the person (a doctor in another state) to whom she owed money that she would pay whatever she could each month until the debt was paid in full. Before the end of the week, her physical symptoms disappeared and now she continues to enjoy her health.

Unfortunately, people often make regrettable mistakes in the reparation process. As Montaigne observed, "The excuses and reparations . . . given to repair indiscretion seem to me more scandalous than the indiscretion itself."

Some guidelines that can be used to prevent unwise approaches to reparation are: (1) Reparation should aim at developing relationships. If attempts at reparation reopen old wounds, add unnecessary burdens to another person, or raise doubts and distrust, then they do more harm than good. One of my clients was told, "If you have a bad thought about a person, you should go to that person and tell him." Needless to say, such action does *not* strengthen relationships. (2) Restitution should never be made simply to relieve ourselves of a sense of guilt. Confession and apology should not be based on a desire for our own emotional satisfaction. Reparation must never be selfish, but rather it must aim to restore, to amend, to enrich.

People often say, "I know what I need to do and I want to do it, but I just can't follow through." We have all experienced this bitter sense of failure of self-sufficiency. "All my life," confessed Seneca, "I have been seeking to climb out of the pit of my besetting sins. And I can't do it. And I never will unless a hand is let down to me to draw me up." As Augustine expressed the problem. "How often have I lashed at my will and cried leap now! And as I said it, it crouched for the leap, and it all but leapt: and yet it did not leap. And the life to which I was accustomed held me more than the life for which I really yearned!" But the most celebrated lament is from Paul who declared, "To will is present with me; but how to perform that which is good I find not. For the good that I would I do not: but the evil which I would not, that I do. . . . O wretched man that I am!" (Rom. 7:18–19, 24).

Is there an answer to this vexing problem? Can we really change? Or is the best we can hope for merely an endless cycle—committing sin, experiencing guilt, repenting, sinning again, and so on?

With all my heart I believe we can change. I believe the Bible's message to us is that if we are not satisfied with the life we are now living, we can have a better one.

How can this happen? To start with, we must become biblically related to God through faith in Christ. This is the start of a new life, an experience often described as "being born again." As Paul wrote, "Therefore if any man be in Christ, he is a new creature: old things are passed away; behold, all things are become new" (2 Cor. 5:17). Next, we develop a new pattern of thinking: "Be ye transformed by the renewal of your mind" (Rom. 12:2). This pattern of thinking includes a totally new way of handling our affections. "Set your affection on things above, not on things on the earth" (Col. 3:2).

When we allow Christ to live his life through us he gives us the insight and power necessary to live the victorious life. To receive his resources we must accept our responsibility to pray, read the Bible, and attend public worship regularly. In thus following Christ, we are led into a life of active service. As forgiven sinners living responsibly and joyfully we learn to think of ourselves, miraculously enough, as Christ's witnesses.

The admonition "repent ye" (Mark 1:15) involves a backward and a forward look. The backward look gives attention to what has to be amended, the forward look to a new direction for living. To make repentance complete, every effort must be made to turn from past sins and look to the future with hopeful expectation. A new life in Christ is available to anyone who will obey his words.

3

Eliminating Feelings of Discouragement

A surprising number of years ago (now that I think about it) before I became deeply involved in the ministry of counseling, I heard an illustration which sounded slightly exaggerated. Now I've changed my opinion. The illustration was about the devil, who, according to the story, advertised his tools for sale. On the date of sale the tools were displayed for public inspection, each being marked with its sale price. Comprising the list were hatred, envy, jealousy, deceit, lying, pride, and so on. Over to one side away from the others was a harmless-looking tool, well-worn but priced much higher than the others.

"What's the name of this tool?" asked one of the purchasers.

"That is discouragement," replied the devil.

"Why have you priced it so high?"

"Because it is more useful to me than the others. I can pry open and get inside a man's heart with that, when I cannot get near him with the other tools. Once I get inside, I can make him do what I choose. It is badly worn because I use it on almost everyone, since few people know it belongs to me."

The devil's price for discouragement was so high that it was never sold. My own experience—personal, as well as with many others over the years—gives sobering witness to the continuing effectiveness of the evil enemy's tool named discouragement.

What Is Discouragement?

According to the dictionary, discouragement means "to weaken the courage or lessen the confidence of; to dishearten." To be discouraged then is to be lacking in courage, to experience an inability to respond adequately to life as we are being called upon to live it.

Discouragement is a mental condition that is damaging to ourselves and to others. And we are wise to confront it, understand it, and correct it. For, as Dr. George W. Truett, the great pastor-author, believed, "Discouragement . . . is not Christian and is displeasing to God."

As Christians we have come into a biblically defined relationship to God in Christ. We have trusted in Christ's atonement for our sins and "if anyone is in Christ, he is a new creation; the old has gone, the new has come!" (2 Cor. 5:17, NIV). The new life in Christ opens the door to adventure, an exciting pilgrimage. As the psalmist David expressed:

> Happy are they who, nerved by thee,
>   set out on pilgrimage!
> When they pass through Wearyglen,
>   fountains flow for their refreshing,
>   blessings rain upon them;
> They are the stronger as they go,
>   till God at last reveals himself in Sion.
>   (Ps. 84:5–7, *Moffatt*)

Nothing compares with being "nerved" by the Lord to follow him in Christian adventure. But note carefully the statement: "When they pass through Wearyglen."

Wearyglen is that place of discouragement and the psalmist does not say *if* they pass through it, but *when.* Sooner or later the Christian pilgrim comes to his Wearyglen. When we're discouraged we describe our condition as "down in the dumps," or "feeling low," or "in the pits." I remember singing as a boy in Sunday school these lines:

> Down in the dumps I'll never go.
> There's where the devil keeps me low.
> So I'll pray with all my might
> To keep my heart all right
> So down in the dumps I'll never go.

Great Christians have experienced discouragement. Bunyan in *Pilgrim's Progress* referred to "the Slough of Despond." The great reformer, Martin Luther, became so discouraged he cried out, "I am sick of life, if that is what you call it." The psalmist David represents all of us at some time or another when he asks, "Why are you downcast, O my soul?" (Ps. 42:5, NIV).

Although discouragement is experienced by the whole person, it is helpful to understand wholeness in terms of its parts—spirit, mind, and body. That is, we experience discouragement spiritually (in our relationship to God), psychologically (in our thoughts and emotions), and physically. In addition we must include other people since, as Paul wrote, "None of us lives to himself alone and none of us dies to himself alone" (Rom. 14:7, NIV). To go a step farther we must understand that each of the three parts of the person affects the other parts and that the person affects and is affected by other people. Sounds complicated, doesn't it? And it is. Perhaps the following diagram will clarify what has been said:

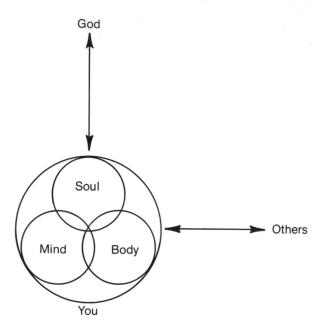

What Are the Signs of Discouragement?

Although space prevents a complete coverage of the many signs of discouragement, brief attention will be given to the following major symptoms:

confusion and indecision
lack of initiative
shrinking back from spiritual activities
social withdrawal
avoidance of responsibility
physical signs (facial expression, voice, tone, posture, etc.)

Confusion and indecision. One of the most common signs of discouragement is a pattern of unclear thinking and an inability to make decisions. This is accompanied by feelings of helplessness and fear and sometimes anger—anger at self, God, and others.

Lack of initiative. Often discouraged persons expect too much of life, others, God, even themselves. Loss of courage results and is linked with lack of initiative. An expectation that fails to understand the importance of willingness to risk, to take the first step, to "make something happen" is bound to be unrealistic.

To live successfully we must dream dreams, set goals, make plans, and act accordingly. But discouragement prevents the development of such a pattern of living. We cannot dream dreams and set goals beyond our ability to believe that we can achieve them. Lack of confidence sets low levels of accomplishment and results in mediocrity. This happens far too often to people as they grow older. Thoreau noted, "The youth gets together his materials to build a bridge to the moon, or perchance a palace or temple on the earth, and at length the middle-aged man concludes to build a woodshed with them."

Shrinking back from spiritual activities. When Christian living makes demands that a person lacks courage to respond to in an adequate way, it is not uncommon for the person to resent God. "Why should this happen to me?" such a person will usually ask and then accuse God of giving burdens too great to bear. This attitude shows in church absenteeism, neglect of Bible reading, praying, and witnessing.

Social withdrawal. Discouragement is always experienced socially. A lack of courage in our interpersonal relationships frequently results in withdrawing from people. Such withdrawal can take a number of forms: being uncommunicative, absenteeism, and unpredictability, to name a few.

Avoidance of responsibility. Acceptance of responsibility requires that we possess the confidence that we can fulfill responsibility. Failing in this confidence causes people to avoid responsibility.

Physical signs of discouragement are well known: sad face, drooping shoulders, slow movement, poor voice tone, halting speech pattern, and so on.

What Causes Discouragement?

Discouragement is not caused by what happens to us, but rather by how we respond to what happens to us. Discouraged people talk about "circumstances" and "facts" that explain their discouragement. They make statements such as, "I can't help it," or "There is nothing I can do." Often they refer regretfully to the past with "If only I . . ." or worriedly to the future with "What if . . . ." The true cause of discouragement then is in the attitude taken toward life—past, present, and future. And this is another way of saying that the cause is wrong, negative, ineffective thinking.

A way of thinking that very often contributes to discouragement is known as emotional reasoning. Victims of emotional reasoning rely on their feelings to interpret reality. Here's the way it can work: It begins with a very negative emotional reaction, perhaps to a thought ("I'm not as smart as I ought to be") or to a disappointment ("I didn't get the job I wanted") or to a rejection ("I've lost a valued relationship"). Now the negative reaction is not what causes discouragement so much as the way we think about it. For example, a client recently described her feelings toward her husband and then concluded, "I can't love him and feel this way about him, can I?"

"Of course," I said, explaining further that our feelings are not under the direct control of our will. All of us experience negative emotional reactions to our world every day. This is perfectly normal. Trouble starts when our negative feelings become our reality, telling us if we're close to God, happy, in love, valuable as persons, etc.

If we allow a negative feeling to determine reality, then our thoughts become negative too. "I don't feel that God loves me" is a negative thought about a negative feeling. And the negative thought makes the negative feeling worse. The result is a vicious circle with the negative feeling leading to negative thinking which makes the feelings more negative. This is not only a vicious circle but it also has a downward spiral. Emotional reasoning is characteristic of discouraged people. They commonly experience what a discouraged client said to me: "I'm in a quagmire and the harder I struggle, the deeper I sink."

A sense of worthlessness. Discouraged people commonly suffer from low self-esteem. They believe that they are unattractive, stupid, unacceptable.

On a recent trip to Hong Kong, Dr. Norman Vincent Peale discovered a tattoo parlor run by an elderly Chinese practitioner of this ancient art. He noticed in the window a display of the various tattoos that could be imprinted on your skin if you were so inclined: flags and patriotic slogans, anchors and daggers, skulls and crossbones, mermaids, and so on. But the one that caught his eye was the phrase *born to lose.* Curious, he approached the owner and, finding that he spoke English, asked if people really requested that such a tattoo be imprinted on themselves.

"Yes," he replied, occasionally they did. The last customer who asked for it had had it imprinted on his chest.

"Why on earth," Dr. Peale asked him, "would anyone want to be branded with a gloomy slogan like that?"

The old Chinese proprietor shrugged and gave this penetrating answer: "Before tattoo on chest, tattoo on mind!"

All of us have tattoo parlors in our minds. When "born to lose" and other self-belittling beliefs are tattooed on the mind, it's no wonder that discouragement shows up in the form of feeling undeserving and worthless.

One of the most common causes of discouragement is failure. Although no one enjoys failing, the act of failure is not nearly as bad as we usually think it is. In fact, when failure is properly understood, it is not something to be avoided. Rather it should be understood as a positive aid. For success is not the absence of failure. We fail our way to success! You don't have to be a baseball fan to remember Babe Ruth, who until recently held the record for hitting home runs. But he also holds another record—more strike-outs than any other player in the history of the sport. Thus the Babe experienced the greatest failure rate in becoming one of baseball's all-time home-run hitters.

And how's this for a record of failure:

lost his job in 1832

failed in business in 1833

lost his sweetheart who died in 1836

suffered a nervous breakdown in 1836

defeated in race for speaker of state legislature in 1838

defeated for nomination to Congress in 1843

rejected as land officer in 1849

defeated in race for U.S. Senate in 1856

lost bid for nomination for U.S. Vice President in 1856

In spite of (perhaps due to) this astonishing record of failures, Abraham Lincoln became president of the United States in 1860.

Methods of Handling Discouragement

1. Learn to encourage yourself. Follow the example of David—king, soldier, poet, saint—one of the greatest men of the Bible. What did he do when his life was

threatened by false accusers? "And David encouraged himself in the Lord his God" (1 Sam. 30:6). How did he encourage himself? He said encouraging things to himself. To get an idea of how David encouraged himself, we can study what he wrote in Psalms. Consider the encouraging effect of the following verses (NIV:)

4:1

> Answer me when I call to you,
>   O my righteous God.
> Give me relief from my distress;
>   be merciful to me and hear my prayer.

8:3–4

> When I consider your heavens,
>   the work of your fingers,
> the moon and the stars,
>   which you have set in place,
> what is man that you are mindful of him,
>   the son of man that you care for him?

27:14

> Wait for the LORD;
>   be strong and take heart
>   and wait for the LORD.

34:17–18

> The righteous cry out, and the LORD hears them;
>   he delivers them from all their troubles.
> The LORD is close to the brokenhearted
>   and saves those who are crushed in spirit.

46:1

> God is our refuge and strength,
> > an ever present help in trouble.

47:7

> For God is the King of all the earth;
> > sing to him a psalm of praise.

57:7

> My heart is steadfast, O God,
> > my heart is steadfast;
> > I will sing and make music.

86:5

> You are kind and forgiving, O Lord,
> > abounding in love to all who call to you.

118:24

> This is the day the LORD has made;
> > let us rejoice and be glad in it.

Now all of us talk to ourselves. The trouble with most of us is that we say the wrong things to ourselves. Discouraged people are often heard making such statements as, "I'm not able," "God won't forgive me," "Everything is going wrong," "Other people are smarter than I," "It's no use trying anymore." It's no wonder that when we think and speak such negative thoughts, we lose courage.

If negative thoughts lead into discouragement, then positive thoughts lead out of and prevent discouragement. Encourage yourself in the Lord by filling your mind with power-packed truths from God's Word, truths that emphasize God's power, promises, love, and nearness to you. Meditate on them, say them out loud, and watch how courage comes flooding into your personality.

Imagine the encouraging power of such thoughts! When the mind is filled with these kinds of truths, personality is energized and elevated. The best self-help program ever discovered is based on developing this positive, Scripture-based pattern of thinking. Begin the day with uplifting thoughts. When negative thoughts enter your mind, quickly replace them with positive thoughts. Cultivate this mentality throughout the day. Before you go to sleep at night make sure that the last waking thoughts are the kind that produce confidence, serenity, and optimism.

"I can do everything through him who gives me strength." So reads one of Christendom's most celebrated quotes, which comes from a letter to a small group of believers living in Philippi (Phil. 4:13, NIV). And Paul's life proved the truth of his bold assertion. The biblical record reveals that after his conversion Paul lived so victoriously, productively, joyfully that he was able to make the claim of confident, adequate living.

How did Paul become such an adequate person? The most obvious answer is found in these words: ". . . through Christ who strengthens me." However, we know that Christ makes himself available to us all. Yet, how many of us experience him strengthening us to the extent that *we* can do all things?

Now the answer that is not so obvious is found in verse 8 of the same chapter: "Finally, brothers, whatever is true, whatever is noble, whatever is right, whatever is pure, whatever is lovely, whatever is admirable—if anything is excellent or praiseworthy—think about such things" (Phil. 4:8, NIV). Paul was able to live successfully because he had learned to *think* successfully. No psychologist ever understood better than Paul the power of thought. The purpose of scriptural meditations is to promote the kind of thinking that leads to victorious Christian living. When read each morning and reflected on during the day, these powerful biblical truths produce miraculous changes in people. For it is when the mind is renewed that we are transformed.

Know who you are. Learn the lesson contained in the following poem.

Who Am I? Who I Am

The world says, "You're nobody . . ."
Jesus says, "I am Somebody, I'm Special, called and chosen of him to a holy calling and to walk in a worthy vocation."
The world said, "You come from nowhere."
Jesus says, "I was created and sent from the presence of the Father."
The world says, "You're poor."
Jesus says, "I'm rich according to his riches in glory."
The world says, "You're ugly!"
Jesus says, "I am beautiful when I let the beauty of Jesus be seen in me."
The world says, "Nobody knows you."
Jesus says, "I knew you before the worlds were formed."
The world says, "You're rejected!"
Jesus says, "I am accepted in the Beloved."
The world says, "I hate you!"
Jesus says, "I love you and gave My life for you that you might have eternal life."
The world says, "You're weak."
Jesus says, "My joy is your strength."
The world says, "You're a failure."
Jesus says, "You can do all things through me, Christ Jesus."
The world says, "You're lonely."
Jesus says, "I will never leave you or forsake you."
The world says, "You have no talents, so what can you do?" And I hung my head and cried,
"Oh Lord, I don't even have a 'one talent.' What about me, Lord?"
Then he answered,
"Ah, my child, ———— listen,
I have given you eyes to behold my beauty,

Ears to hear the symphony of music played by my creation.

I have given you a tongue to tell of my love;

Lips to kiss away the hurts of childhood, and to transmit words of comfort to the uncomforted.

The hands I have given you are to serve your fellowman, and with which to create beauty.

Your shoulders on which to balance the burdens of others.

I have given you a heart to care with, feet to speed the spread of my Good News;

A mind that I can fill with my thoughts, your fingers to write them down, so that you might share them with others."

Alas, my heart broke with contrition,

"Forgive me, Lord, forgive me!"

For I realized not a "one talent," but many had he given me,

TO USE FOR MY MASTER'S GLORY!

—Anonymous

Remind yourself of help received in the past. In his fascinating autobiography entitled *My Pilgrimage*, Dr. F. W. Boreham recalls an episode from his childhood that made a lasting impression on his highly productive life. In his childhood home a framed text plainly printed on a scrap of white paper cut from the cover of an almanac hung on the wall of his mother's bedroom for fifty years. It was more highly valued than the finest pictures in the house and read like this:

HITHERTO

HATH

THE LORD

HELPED US

When Dr. Boreham and his brother pressed for an explanation, Mrs. Boreham shared this with her sons: "You know that Father and I had a crushing trouble and we feared a much heavier one. On Tuesday of last week I was feeling dreadfully worried. I do not know why I felt it so terribly just then, but I did. I had to drop my work, pick up the baby, and walk up and down the kitchen feeling that I could endure it all no longer. My burden was heavier than I could bear: it seemed to be killing me. In pacing up and down I paused for a second in front of the almanac on the wall. The only thing I saw was the text in the corner. I felt as if it had been put there specially for me. It was as if some one had spoken the words. 'Hitherto hath the Lord helped us.' I was so overcome that I sat down and had a good cry; and then I began again with fresh heart and trust. When Father came home I told him all about it, and he cut out the text with his penknife, had it framed, and hung it where you now see it."

One of the best ways to find encouragement is to help someone else, as pointed out by an anonymous poet:

How to Be Happy

Are you almost disgusted with life, little man?
  I'll tell you a wonderful trick
That will bring you contentment, if anything can,
  Do something for somebody, quick!

Are you awfully tired with play, little girl?
  Wearied, discouraged, and sick—
I'll tell you the loveliest game in the world,
  Do something for somebody, quick!

Though it rains, like the rain of the flood, little man,
  And the clouds are forbidding and thick,
You can make the sun shine in your soul, little man,
  Do something for somebody, quick!

Though the stars are like brass overhead, little girl,
  And the walls like a well-heated brick,
And our earthly affairs in a terrible whirl,
  Do something for somebody, quick!

—Anonymous

Learn to live today. Such counsel seems self-evident, doesn't it? But too few of us live today. Most people live in the two worst days of the week: yesterday and tomor-

row. We need the encouragement found in God's promise to his people when they were faced with the task of
conquering a new land: "As thy days [meaning as thy
todays], so shall thy strength be" (Deut. 33:25).

Life can be faced—today. And the biblical promise as-
sures us strength for today. We must learn the poet's
insight:

> Yard by yard
>   Life is hard.
> Inch by inch
>   It's a cinch.

That is, we can face whatever comes, if we take it one
day at a time. This includes those challenges that we
might have thought too great for us to handle. But we
discover that new situations call forth new power—
power that we didn't realize we had.

Someone once asked D. L. Moody if he had dying
grace. "No," he replied, "now I have living grace, but
when I come to die I shall be given dying grace." He had
learned that God gives us today what he knows we need
to enable us to stand life's test. As the poet says:

> God broke the years to hours and days
> That hour by hour
> And day by day,
> Just going on a little way,
> We might be able all along
> To keep quite strong.
>
> —George Kingle

As thy days, so shall thy strength be (Deut. 33:25).

When discouragement begins to set in, remember
some of the great names in history and the obstacles they
faced and overcame. Beethoven composed his inspiring
music even though he was deaf. Sir Walter Scott wrote
his classic tales as he limped through life. John Milton,

author of *Paradise Lost*, was blind, as was Homer, the brilliant Greek poet.

As a writer I've found encouragement from learning that Louisa May Alcott, author of *Little Women*, was told by an editor that she had no talent to write and was advised to stick to her sewing. And when Walt Disney submitted his first drawings for publication, the editor told him he had no artistic ability. Thomas Edison's teachers sent him home with a note telling his parents that their son was too stupid to learn. F. W. Woolworth at twenty-one years of age was not allowed to wait on the customers in the store where he worked. His employers told him he didn't have enough sense to meet the public. But he built a great chain of stores.

Robert Louis Stevenson wrote literature read and enjoyed by millions. The beloved author of *Treasure Island* admitted, "For 14 years I have not had a day's real health," yet he could add, "I have written in bed . . . out of it, written in hemorrhages . . . torn by coughing . . . when my head swam for weakness." His radiant faith is expressed in this prayer: "We thank thee . . . for the hope with which we expect the morrow; for the health, the work, the food, and the bright skies . . . our friends in all parts of the earth . . . give us the strength to encounter that which is to come, that we may be brave in peril . . . temperate in wrath . . . and down to the gates of death, loyal and loving to one another."

The reason Stevenson could live such a productive, overcoming life is found in this remarkable philosophy: "As yesterday is history, and tomorrow may never come, I have resolved from this day on, I will do all the business I can honestly, have all the fun I can reasonably, do all the good I can willingly, and save my disposition by thinking pleasantly."

Associate with encouraging people. Here we are reminded of one of the great responsibilities of the church. Discouraged people need fellowship with believers heeding the admonition of Paul, those who "try to excel in

gifts that build up [strengthen, encourage] the church"
(1 Cor. 14:12, NIV). When the church is truly the encouraging fellowship that it ought to be, discouraged people
can find new strength and courage. Regular attendance
with this kind of Christian fellowship, service, and worship can do wonders.

The head of a large hospital faced an epidemic when
her staff was short. Nearing the point of exhaustion, one
day she said to a subordinate: "I'm all in. I must consult a
nerve specialist or [and she did not know why she said it]
else go to church." She did go to church and there she
found new courage.

Keep on keeping on. Persist as Paul exhorted the Gala-
tians: "Let us not become weary in doing good, for at the
proper time we will reap a harvest, if we do not give up"
(6:9, NIV).

> When things go wrong, as they sometimes will,
> When the road you're trudging seems all uphill,
> When the funds are low and the debts are high,
> And you want to smile, but you have to sigh,
> When care is pressing you down a bit—
> Rest if you must, but don't you quit.
>
> Life is queer with its twists and turns,
> As every one of us sometimes learns,
> And many a fellow turns about
> When he might have won had he stuck it out.
> Don't give up though the pace seems slow—
> You may succeed with another blow.
>
> Success is failure turned inside out—
> The silver tint of the clouds of doubt,
> And you never can tell how close you are,
> It may be near when it seems afar;
> So stick to the fight when you're hardest hit—
> It's when things seem worst that you musn't quit.
>   —Anonymous

Remember that Jesus is alive. Christianity is different
from all other religions in that it is a way of life based on

hope. No matter what our present condition is, we possess a future expectation that encourages us to persevere. This is forever grounded in the resurrection of Christ. He is alive! That truth gives us the opportunity to have a relationship with him that provides the hope and courage necessary to face and overcome every trial of life.

This truth is illustrated by one of my favorite stories about a Chinese man named Lo. He became a Christian and started reading the New Testament for the first time. When he read the last verse in the Book of Matthew, he was so thrilled that he rushed to tell a friend, excitedly, "The Lord Jesus wrote this for me because he said, 'Lo, I am with you alway.' " When with Lo we realize that the great and precious words of Christ were written for us personally, and that he is with us "alway," we can find the courage to live triumphantly.

We have scriptural evidence for believing that we can overcome life's hardships, disappointments, failures, losses. Christians realize that they are not always spared life's tribulations. Consider the testimony of Saint Paul:

> . . . five times received I forty stripes save one. Thrice was I beaten with rods, once was I stoned, thrice I suffered shipwreck, a night and a day I have been in the deep; In journeyings often, in perils of waters, in perils of robbers, in perils by mine own countrymen, in perils by the heathen, in perils in the city, in perils in the wilderness, in perils in the sea, in perils among false brethren; In weariness and painfulness, in watchings often, in hunger and thirst, in fastings often, in cold and nakedness (2 Cor. 11:24–27).

In spite of all his trials, Paul kept his hope and courage. He chose to relate himself to Christ, drawing from his resources and trusting his promises. Because of this, he could write to the Christians in Rome, "No one who believes in him will ever be disappointed . . . no one" (Rom. 10:11, *Moffatt*).

4

Overcoming Fears and Worries

Life is best lived when we're conscious of becoming all that we're capable of becoming.

We all want this successful pattern of living, but so few have it. How do we achieve it? One of the principles that we can use to guide us to the answer is this: Our personal development and success in life are determined by our attitudes toward life's realities.

We experience these realities through the God-given gift of imagination. This precious function of the mind has enormous power to inspire, direct, and strengthen us in daily living. The positive uses of imagined reality are faith, hope, and love.

However, it is more common to use our imagination negatively. The negative uses of imagined reality are commonly known as fear, phobia, and worry. This "terrible trio" blocks growth, generates personality disturbance, and makes life miserable.

We are responsible for our attitudes, so by negatively imagining reality we hinder our own progress. The late Walt Kelly's comic-strip character, Pogo, was right when he said, "We have met the enemy and they is us!"

Some of our greatest thinkers have wrestled with how to help people become what they are capable of becoming. Consider what two of them have said. "The first duty of man is that of subduing fear," said Thomas Carlyle. "We must get rid of fear; we cannot act at all till then." And Ralph Waldo Emerson said, "He has not learned the lesson of life who does not every day surmount a fear."

The purpose of this chapter is to enable you to learn the lesson of life and daily overcome your fears and worries as well. For many years I have worked as a Christian specialist in mental health. During this time I have witnessed that Christian faith based on biblical understanding provides us with all we need to master our fears and phobias and to overcome every worry.

Fear

One of the most dangerous characteristics of fear is that our fears often are self-fulfilling. Job, after losing his family, his fortune, and his health, lamented, "For the thing I greatly feared has come upon me." He added, "What I dreaded has happened to me" (3:25, ARV). Frequently I have heard clients refer to various personal misfortunes and sigh, "I was afraid that would happen" or "The things I fear have a way of coming to pass." How often our fears bring about the very thing we feared would happen.

A student fears he will fail an exam and he does. An employee fears he will lose his job and he's fired. Fear of not being liked leads to more insecurity. Fear of failing leads to indecision, or procrastination. The pattern is familiar. A person begins to imagine "What if such and such happens?" Fear leads to dread, accompanied by worry and anxiety. Before long nervousness and fatigue set in. Sleepless nights and miserable days combine to cause collapse. From the Old Testament comes this pungent reminder: "He that fleeth from the fear shall fall into the pit" (Jer. 48:44).

Fear is also connected to doubt. William Shakespeare identified the tragic relationship:

> Our doubts are traitors,
> And make us lose the good we oft might win,
> By fearing to attempt.
> —*Measure for Measure* (I. iv. 78)

By doubting ("I can't do it," "I might fail") I fear to make the attempt. How many great and good deeds have never been done because fear prevented action?

Foes or Friends?

Our fears are either our enemies or our allies. As our enemies, fears stifle creativity, block growth, and create misery. Study the brief earthly ministry of Jesus as recorded by Matthew, Mark, Luke, and John and you will find him spending much of his time helping people with their fears. His conversations were punctuated with the words *fear, anxious,* and *troubled.* Such statements as "fear not," "be not over anxious," and "let not your heart be troubled, neither let it be afraid" were made to those he loved.

But fears have a positive value also. They can teach us, motivate us to grow, and cause us to learn life's most important lessons.

Our fear is an ally when it protects us against danger. In *Moby Dick*, Starbuck, the mate on the *Pequod*, states passionately, "I'll have no man in my boat who does not fear a whale."

To learn to fear what ought to be feared is an important part of our education. This type of fear motivates us to drive safely, eat sensibly, exercise regularly—to do whatever protects and sustains life.

But there are other kinds of benefits too. A student studies harder when he fears failure. Before he chooses a mate, a young person uses caution and seeks counseling because he fears the consequences of a wrong choice. A man buys insurance because he fears leaving his family without enough money to provide for their material needs.

However, the most constructive fear is "the fear of the LORD." This fear "is the beginning of wisdom" (Ps. 111:10). In Psalm 33:8 we read, "Let all the earth fear the LORD: let all the inhabitants of the world stand in awe of him." This kind of fear means reverence, awe, and respect. It becomes a positive force in our lives, enabling us to make better choices and direct our lives according to principles of meaningful, productive, and joyful living.

Fear becomes our ally when we use it as a spur to resist temptation. Granted, there are "pleasures [in] sin for a season" (Heb. 11:25). But, as a familiar warning reminds us, "Be not deceived; God is not mocked: for whatsoever a man soweth, that shall he also reap. For he that soweth to his flesh shall of the flesh reap corruption; but he that soweth to the Spirit shall of the Spirit reap life everlasting" (Gal. 6:7–8). We are wise to fear the consequences of wrongdoing.

We have reassurance that when we do succumb to temptation and sin, God forgives us: "If we confess our sins, he is faithful and just to forgive us our sins, and to cleanse us from all unrighteousness" (1 John 1:9). Repentance repairs our relationship with God but does not eliminate the consequences of our wrongdoing. This knowledge should produce a healthy fear. It also motivates us to get a better understanding of temptation.

Thomas à Kempis described the steps of temptation: "First there cometh to mind a base thought of evil, then a strong imagination thereof, afterward a delight and evil motive, and then consent."

Fear becomes our friend when we use it to confront the temptation when it first enters our mind. As a Chinese proverb states, "We cannot keep the birds from flying over our heads but we can keep them from building a nest thereon!" It's not what goes into the mind but what stays inside that leads to desire and eventually action. Fear can be used to replace the wrong thought before it gains too much strength. Love and wisdom will find the proper substitute. Among the biblical statements that teach us the positive, growth-producing effects of the right kind of fear are the following:

By the fear of the LORD men depart from evil (Prov. 16:6).

The fear of the LORD tendeth to life: and he that hath it shall abide satisfied; he shall not be visited with evil (Prov. 19:23).

By faith Noah, being divinely warned of things not yet seen, moved with godly fear, prepared an ark for the saving of his household (Heb. 11:7, ARV).

Six Basic Fears

Over the years many writers have presented their thoughts on the kinds of fears we have. One of these authors, Napoleon Hill, identifies six basic fears:

fear of poverty
fear of criticism
fear of ill health
fear of loss of love
fear of old age
fear of death

All of us experience these fears in varying ways and degrees.

Life's most important decisions are our choice of a mate, a life's work, becoming parents, and preparation for death. Fear of failing in these great decisions should lead to better educational preparation, greater self-knowledge, caution, balanced living, and above all wisdom. We are not really ready to live unless we are ready to die. A healthy fear of entering eternity unprepared can lead us to life's greatest decision: to accept Christ's gift of salvation. In this chapter we will see how faith and love become even stronger than fear in their power to help us live obedient Christian lives.

Phobias

Phobias are exaggerated, persistent fears. A few of the most common are acrophobia (fear of heights), agoraphobia (fear of open spaces; the most common—one in twenty experience it), claustrophobia (fear of closed places), herpetophobia (fear of reptiles), ochlophobia (fear of crowds), and thanatophobia (fear of death).

Recently a lead article in *Newsweek* was "The Fight to Conquer Fear." The article focused on phobias, defining phobia as "fear looking at itself in the mirror." Calling phobias "the disease of the decade," the writer points out that what schizophrenia was to the 1960s, what depression and burnout were to the 1970s, phobias are to the 1980s.

According to a survey to be published by the National Institute of Mental Health, one in nine adults suffers with some kind of phobia. Phobias are second only to alcoholism as the nation's leading mental-health problem.

Phobias create a sense of panic, symptoms of which are sweaty palms, heart palpitations, dizziness, "butterflies," "weak knees," or shortness of breath. In its most severe form this kind of personality disturbance is called a panic attack. People who have phobias fear that these symptoms will occur, especially in public. Their fear and embarrassment lead to avoidance behavior that restricts their activity to an alarming degree. This can cause inconvenience, social withdrawal, or elaborate manipulation to avoid the things that cause panic.

Worry

Worry and fear are linked together. Worry results from negatively anticipating the future. It is characterized by "what-if" thinking.

> Worry gives you something to do.
> It's like a rocking chair.
> You are in it, it is true,
> But it never takes you anywhere!
> —Louis O. Caldwell

Worry is a nonconstructive mental activity, and commonly takes such forms as these:

What if I lose everything? (fear of poverty)

What if I fall short of others' expectations? (fear of criticism)

What if I get sick? (fear of ill health)

What if my spouse leaves me? (fear of loss of love)

What if I can't take care of myself when I grow old? (fear of old age)

What if I'm not prepared to die? (fear of death)

Some time ago archaeologists in Britain uncovered a cliff that had been buried for centuries. It showed that ancient men, too, had fears and worries. To portray their inner disturbances, they drew pictures of a gigantic wolf sinking its teeth into the neck of a man.

Interestingly enough, the word *worry* is derived from an Old English word meaning "to strangle" or "to choke." By the wrong use of our minds we allow fear and worry to put a strangle hold on our creative ability.

After returning from a vacation, Norman Vincent Peale found 1,633 requests for prayer on his desk. As he went through the letters, one by one, he began to notice that most of them specifically mentioned worry, implied it, or reflected it. More than two-thirds of the writers were afraid and worried. What were they worried about? Ranking first was worry about money: how to cope with inflation, pay bills, pay taxes, or finance a home. Ranking a close second was worry about health. The third worry was about someone else: a wife worrying about her husband, a husband worrying about his wife, or parents worrying about their children.

A group of 104 psychologists went through their case studies and found that specific worries are common at particular ages. At eighteen we worry about ideals and personal appearance; at twenty about appearance; at twenty-three about moods; at twenty-six about making a good impression; at thirty about salary and the cost of living; at thirty-one about business success; at thirty-three about job security; at thirty-eight about health; at forty-one about politics; at forty-two about marital problems; at forty-five about the loss of ambition; over fifty-five about health.

Amazingly, we waste our worries on troubles that rarely materialize. As wise old Emerson observed,

> Some of your hurts you have cured,
>   And the sharpest you still have survived,
> But what torments of grief you endured
>   From evils which never arrived!

Our destructive fears and worries are bad enough but a deeper look into our attitudes reveals a greater enemy. This enemy is greater than our fears and worries because it lies deeper in our nature. It is an unlearned, inborn tendency to be susceptible to negative influences.

The tendency cannot be understood and dealt with logically. The problem and the solution are deeper. Perhaps the clearest expression of this human dilemma is found in a letter to a group of Christians in Rome. Consider what the writer, one of the world's most brilliant thinkers, means when he confesses: "I do not understand what I do. For what I want to do I do not do, but what I hate I do. . . . For I have the desire to do what is good, but I cannot carry it out" (Rom. 7:15, 18, NIV). What makes this enemy even more dangerous is how it can disguise itself. It can attack from without in the form of adverse circumstances and negative influences of others, usually those we love and admire the most. Or it can attack from within in the form of fears, worry, anxiety, or distress of personality. Such incapacitating states frequently weaken and disturb the self. What can we do about this enemy within?

We look in vain for adequate answers to this perplexing problem unless we go to the Scriptures. There we find the truth about ourselves. No other book in the world reveals us to ourselves as does the Bible. No other book comes close in providing tested authority for people seeking solutions to their problems.

An Important Distinction

It's important to distinguish between a fear reaction that is emotional and a response that is behavioral. As an emotional reaction fear is normal, even desirable. We are constructed so that we experience emotional reactions to thoughts, circumstances, and uncertainty. These emotions are not under the control of the will and can produce a state of tension, nervousness, or anger. These emotional reactions are frequently accompanied by physical symptoms. No one ever expressed this reaction better than did David: "Fearfulness and trembling are come upon me, and horror hath overwhelmed me. And I said, Oh that I had wings like a dove! for then would I fly away, and be at rest" (Ps. 55:5–6).

As a behavioral response, fear is one of our greatest enemies to successful, productive living. I use the term *behavioral* because it is vital to understand that it is not what we feel but what we do or refuse to do with the feeling that counts. This feeling of fear causes people to seek to escape responsibility, temptation, challenge, risk, or conflict.

How to Be an Overcomer

Face your fears. When I began to receive invitations to speak in various areas of the country, I had a problem. I was scared of flying. Before each flight I requested prayer in every church in Houston where I lived. I imagined everything that could go wrong. I was miserable.

Finally I made a decision. I had read that the only way to overcome a fear is to face it. "Do the thing you fear and the death of that fear is certain." So I began to take flying lessons. After eight or nine hours of training I soloed, and it was great! A short time later I was licensed as a private pilot. Now, flying is one of the great thrills of my life.

Ask yourself: What is the worst that could happen? The pilots in the First World War faced their fears and worries by thinking, "When you are in the air you will be flying straight or turning over. If you are flying straight, there is no cause to worry. If you are turning over, one of two things is true; you will right the plane or fall. If you right the plane, there is no cause to worry. If you fall, one of two things is certain; you will be injured slightly or seriously. If you are injured slightly, there is no need to worry. If you are injured seriously, one of two things will happen: you will die or recover. If you recover, there is no need to worry, and if you die, you can't."

Use the rule of three. One of the most helpful things to do when fear, phobias, and worry unleash emotional storms is to apply the rule of three. This psychological technique is to face the fear and do what is feared no matter how mutinous the emotions become. Then you do it a second time. You may feel like "passing out" or "falling apart" or "dying a thousand deaths" but now you have the assurance that you actually did this before and survived the ordeal. With the third attempt your confidence begins to soar and your behavior is controlled more by your mind than your emotions. By applying the rule of three you learn that it is all right to feel the agony of fear. You learn that the agony is temporary and that it yields to action. "Do what you fear and the death of that fear is certain."

*Seek counseling.** When the cause of fear and worry is known, the cure is already on its way. Talking with a skilled counselor can be an effective way to recognize the origin of the problems. After the cause is identified, however, biblical principles need to be applied so that the problem can be overcome.

As I was writing this chapter, my telephone rang. The caller wanted to talk to me about his wife, whose fears had overcome her. He brought her to see me and she was so panicky that she couldn't speak. What made the problem worse was her attitude that "I'm a Christian and I shouldn't feel like this!"

This woman's fears were rooted in her childhood. Her father had sexually abused her a number of times when she was a little girl. She was afraid to tell anyone and had carried her torment into adulthood. Finally the fears had surfaced in the form of frequent tears, excessive sleep, social withdrawal, and resentment toward God.

In our counseling sessions she finally was able to talk about her bitter childhood experiences. She faced her fears, understood them, and received scriptural counseling. This along with loving support from her husband had produced the desired result.

Use fear to motivate you to do whatever you fear. A certain man was developing a business that required learning to relate to people. He was afraid of people. But he had a greater fear—working forty more years for the company where he was employed at that time! Thus he made creative use of fear by considering the alternative to being afraid of relating to people. If you have a fear that's keep-

*See chapter 9.

ing you from reaching your goal, learn to use the fear in a positive way.

Overcome fear with love. The apostle John wrote, "There is no fear in love; but perfect love casteth out fear: because fear hath torment. He that feareth is not made perfect in love" (1 John 4:18). Is he contradicting other biblical writers who believed in the positive effects of fear? The Bible never contradicts itself. Truth cannot be nontruth, and the Bible is the inspired revelation without error. Also, John makes it clear that he is writing about fear "that hath torment." Fear that torments, disrupts, fragments, weakens, or poisons can be overcome in only one way, the way of perfect love.

Let's begin by seeking to understand this perfect love, its exalted position, its pattern, its power, and how it behaves. Paul has given us this vital information in 1 Corinthians 13. The inspired writer begins by showing that love is superior to sacrificial giving: "And though I bestow all my goods to feed the poor, and though I give my body to be burned, and have not charity [love], it profiteth me nothing" (v. 3).

Next, Paul describes the beautiful pattern of perfect love (v. 4). "Love suffers long" (it is patient); "is kind" (it behaves toward others with sensitivity); "envieth not, . . . vaunteth not itself, is not puffed up" (it has no "chip on its shoulder," is not bothered by the success or good fortune of others, and has the ego under control).

This love does not "behave itself unseemly, seeketh not her own" (it behaves appropriately with an unselfish concern for others); "is not easily provoked, thinketh no evil" (it shows self-control, refusing to be resentful when mistreated); "rejoiceth not in iniquity, but rejoiceth in the truth" (it distinguishes the right and the wrong and takes pleasure in the truth; vv. 5–6).

More positively, perfect love "beareth all things," "believeth all things" (it is not gullible but chooses to believe, instead of being skeptical or cynical); "hopeth all things" (it responds positively to the future as promised by God's Word); "endureth all things" (it has the courage to face life; v. 7).

Perfect love behaves according to this remarkable pattern. It rises above life's conflicts and challenges not only in its responses and reactions, but also in its quality and manner. No wonder Paul could say love "never faileth" (v. 8).

The three values that outlast all the others are faith, hope, and love. The *power* of perfect love is seen in Paul's conclusion that "the greatest of these is charity" (v. 13).

How Do We Develop Love?

We have seen that perfect love enables us to overcome self-defeating fear. Now let's examine how to develop this perfect love. Study carefully this advice: "Add to your faith virtue; and to virtue knowledge; and to knowledge temperance; and to temperance patience; and to patience godliness; and to godliness brotherly kindness; and to brotherly kindness charity" (2 Peter 1:5–7).

A clear understanding of how love is developed by adding virtue to virtue corrects the mistaken idea that Christian love can be easily and quickly taken on at conversion. As someone has said, "The Christian life must not be an initial spasm followed by chronic inertia."

We make the right start in developing this perfect love when we begin with faith. Faith is defined as "the substance of things hoped for, the evidence of things not seen" (Heb. 11:1). Without faith we cannot please God (Heb. 11:6). Every man has been given a measure of faith. We don't need to ask for more faith. What we need to do is illustrated by an incident which took place in a restaurant in Washington during World War II. A customer who had already received his share of sugar (a rationed commodity) demanded more for his coffee. "Stir what you've got!" replied the waitress. Her advice applies to our requests for more faith. We need to learn to "stir what we've got"!

To faith we must add virtue or courage. True faith leads to courageous living as active witnesses of the Christ we serve.

To courage there must be added knowledge. With this kind of knowledge a person makes wise decisions. He applies this wisdom as a practical way to deal with the opportunities and challenges of daily living.

To practical knowledge we must add temperance or self-control. This is the ability to get a grip on oneself. Such self-mastery is not an extinguishing of passion and desire, but rather their reasonable control and direction through enlightened and empowered reason.

To this self-control we then add patience or steadfastness. Christian steadfastness enables a person to go beyond accepting and enduring life to using even the worst experience as a steppingstone to something better. The writer of Hebrews said that "for the joy that was set before him [Christ] endured the cross, despising the shame" (12:2).

To steadfastness we add godliness or piety. This virtue is characteristic of a person who is in a biblically defined relationship with God and his fellow man.

To godliness we add brotherly kindness. Most readers know someone who is "so heavenly minded that he is no earthly good." A good friend of mine tells how Charles Lindbergh completed his solo flight across the Atlantic. When Lindbergh landed, he was asked, "How did you do it?" "It was easy," he replied. "I was by myself."

Some things in life are easier when they are done alone. But as my friend goes on to say, "It's tougher to do it together, but together is more enjoyable." Brotherly kindness seeks involvement with others through the claims, inconveniences, and requirements that relationships demand.

These virtues culminate in Christian love. This love is

from God and is without condition. It is given without regard for the desire for it or the response to it. Christ said, "Love your enemies and pray for those who persecute you" (Matt. 5:44, RSV). Such love for others enables us to overcome our fears of people. And when we love God with all our heart, we lose our fears that come when we know we are not in a right relationship with him.

Another friend shared the following quote with some business associates in Hawaii:

> Love makes you feel special. It changes everyone for the better. It's the one commodity that multiplies when you give it away. The more you spread it around, the more you're able to hold on to it. It keeps coming back to you over and over.
>
> Where love is concerned, it pays to be an absolute spendthrift. It cannot be bought or sold, so give it away. Throw it away. Splash it all over. Empty your pockets and shake the basket. Turn it upside down and shower it on everybody, even those who don't deserve it. You may startle them into behaving in a way you never dreamed possible.
>
> Not only is love the sweet mystery of life, but it's the most powerful motivator known to mankind.

How to Strengthen Your Faith

Remember the example of Christ's disciples. The strength of fear can be seen in the lives of the men Jesus first picked to carry out his mission on earth. Despite his backing, reassurance, and companionship, they all forsook him in his greatest hour of trial. Their fears overcame them all.

Yet Christ never forsook them. One of the first things he did after his resurrection was to seek them out and reassure them once again. As time passed, their courage increased. Jesus ascended to heaven to sit at his Father's right hand. But his reality remained and grew stronger by the Holy Spirit's continued ministry to the disciples left behind to fulfill his purpose.

In the Book of Acts, we read of the rapid growth of the young church, led by inspired disciples. But persecution soon threatened them. Would they run away again as they had when their master was so cruelly taken away? In her devotional booklet, *Power*, Dorothy Hayes gives an inspired answer:

> James, the brother of Jesus, and James the son of Zebedee, were killed by mobs in Jerusalem; Matthew was slain on a sword in Ethiopia; Philip was hanged in Phrygia; Bartholomew flayed alive in Armenia; Andrew crucified in Achaia; Thomas was run through with a lance in East India; Thaddeus was shot to death with arrows; a cross went up in Persia for Simon the Zealot; and in Rome, the old apostle Peter was, at his own request, crucified head downward—because he did not think himself worthy to die in the same position as his Lord. Matthias was beheaded. . . .
>
> A fair record for eleven weaklings who once ran to hide!

Only one of Jesus' first disciples escaped a violent death. That was John, the beloved, who lived out his last years in exile on the island of Patmos.

How did these disciples overcome those fears and become such great men of courage? The answer is given us by another courageous believer, who writes that by their *faith* men have

subdued kingdoms

wrought righteousness

obtained promises

stopped the mouths of lions

quenched the violence of fire

escaped the edge of the sword

out of weakness were made strong

waxed valiant in fight (Heb. 11:33–34)

Increase your faith by attending regular public worship where the Word of God is preached. George W. Comstock, professor of epidemiology at Johns Hopkins University, studied the medical records of five hundred men aged forty-five to sixty-four and concluded that men who attended church at least once a week fell victim to fatal heart disease only half as often as men who were irregular in church attendance. There is no denying the healing, health-giving effects of regular public worship. When with our Christian friends we worship God with our praise and listen to his preached word our faith increases and fears are overcome.

Constantly remind yourself of the source of your help. In the Old Testament we read: "For I the LORD thy God will hold thy right hand, saying unto thee, Fear not; I will help thee" (Isa. 41:13).

And from the New Testament we receive this encouragement: "For God hath not given us the spirit of fear; but of power, and of love, and of a sound mind" (2 Tim. 1:7).

Learn to take every need to God (memorize this). "Don't worry over anything whatever; tell God every detail of your needs in earnest and thankful prayer, and the peace of God, which transcends human understanding, will keep constant guard over your hearts and minds as they rest in Christ Jesus" (Phil. 4:6–7, *Phillips*).

Daily place yourself under the positive influences of people, books, tapes, music, and environments that inspire. Take more responsibility for controlling your life. Deliberately seek out those influences that starve your fears, phobias, and worries and that feed your faith.

Grow in your ability to exercise a positive use of imagined reality and experience the liberty of overcoming your fears, phobias, and worries. From this moment begin to get out of your own way of becoming that productive, successful, and enjoyable person you were meant to be. You can do it!

5

Developing a Positive Self-Image

We all need to pray with the old Scotsman, "Oh, Lord, give me a high opinion of myself."

The reason for such a prayer is found in every human heart. Perhaps we have no greater need that proves the truth of the psalmist David's ancient insight: "He fashioneth [our] hearts alike" (Ps. 33:15). Without exception, every son and daughter of Adam experiences the need for self-esteem, "a high opinion of myself." We need to know that we matter, that we have personal worth and dignity. This need for a healthy, positive regard for ourselves is, according to an ever-growing amount of evidence, one of the deepest needs of our nature.

Tragically enough, however, the vast majority of us suffer greatly the effects of a negative self-image. Why is the negative self-image so common? What *is* self-image? How does it develop? What are the effects of its development? And, perhaps most important, how can the negative self-image be overcome?

The purpose of this chapter is to present in nontechnical language a brief, biblically based attempt to help the reader find a clear, strong, and enduring answer to the old Scot's prayer for his own life.

In my years as a Christian mental-health specialist, I cannot recall a single client who did not have a negative self-image. The writings of experts in the field of counseling support this:

The hardest thing for human beings to do is to know themselves and to change themselves. (Alfred Adler)

Morals, standards, values, or right and wrong behavior are all ultimately related to the fulfillment of our needs for self-worth. (William Glasser)

If I were to search for the central core of difficulty in people as I have come to know them, it is that in the great majority of cases they despise themselves, regarding themselves worthless and unlovable. (Carl R. Rogers)

When a person suffers loss of self-respect he will experience what Sören Kierkegaard called "sickness unto death." This phrase describes a person despairing over his inability to feel a sense of worth. Frequently this despair is communicated through complaints about physical pain or adverse circumstances. Rarely does the person express the real problem. Most people will not admit, "I despise myself. This person that I am fills me with disgust and despair." Instead they walk among us with a terrible burden of quiet desperation, living the "dying life."

The Meaning and Importance of Self-Image

In nontechnical language, our self-image is what we think and feel about ourselves. How vital the self-image is can be understood when we realize this startling truth: Our self-image is lived out as true whether it really is true or not! Our attitude toward ourselves places limits on our ability to set goals, make decisions, choose friends, and perform the tasks of daily living.

Even more sobering is the knowledge that our beliefs about ourselves control our interpretations of our experiences. This means that our beliefs tend to be confirmed by the way we interpret what happens to us. For example, perhaps a person enters a room full of ten people and nine are friendly but one is not. If a person believes that he is not liked, he will block out the nine friendly responses and focus on the negative response. He will leave thinking, "Just as I suspected, those people don't like me." What he believed was confirmed by his highly limiting interpretation of his experience. Each confirmation strengthens the related belief over a period of time; consequently, the self-image becomes more and more difficult to change. But no matter how negative a person's self-image has become, it can be changed.

Development of the Self-Image

The image that we have of ourselves is learned. It is not inherited and we do not "naturally" have one. How we learn who we are might be understood by knowing that we are not who we think we are. Nor are we who others think we are. We are who we think others think we are!

Our self-image, then, is formed in our interactions with other people, most important of whom are our parents. Whether our parents are perceived as sources of need satisfaction or need frustration lays the foundation in our early years for the development of the self-image. What we think they think about us is learned through countless messages communicated in many different ways—facial expression, tone of voice, and behavior (especially physical ways of showing love).

The effects of early influences have been observed and analyzed by many students, parents, and professionals. Over the years we have learned that

> If a child receives encouragement,
>   he learns confidence.
> If a child receives praise,
>   he learns he can do things well.
> If a child receives acceptance,
>   he learns he is acceptable.

If a child receives discipline,
   he learns to discipline himself.
If a child receives love,
   he learns he is lovable.
If a child receives predictability from adults,
   he learns to be secure.

As our social world expands, other people can have great influence on the formation of our self-image. In addition to parents and brothers and sisters, "significant others" such as grandparents and relatives, teachers, ministers, neighbors, and peers play an important part in our social world.

What we think these significant people think about us forms the image of ourselves that we learn, accept, and live out. Since no one lives in a perfect social world, what we learn about ourselves is not totally accurate. We are imperfect persons growing up with imperfect persons, so the self-image develops imperfectly. But since it is learned, it can be changed. And that change can begin when a person decides he wants to change.

Causes of Negative Self-Image

A major reason so many people disapprove of themselves is that we live in a negatively oriented society.

For example, on his first day in school Johnny was asked his name.

"Johnny don't," he answered.

"Johnny don't! What do you mean?" asked the teacher.

"Well," said Johnny, "at home my mother says, 'Johnny, don't do this' and 'Johnny, don't do that.' So I guess that's my name."

Such parenting is an expression of our culture's negativism and is all too common.

Then, consider negative influences in school. Remember your test papers? What did your teacher emphasize? Your good answers? Only the wrong answers received a critical evaluation—usually written in red ink!

Recently a poll was conducted to see if people who attend church receive help in learning to overcome their negative self-image. The results showed that church attendance is not highly related to the development of a positive self-image. Indeed, in too many instances church-related experiences produce a loss of self-esteem.

Negative emphases in home, school, and church—little wonder that by the time we reach adulthood our self-images are usually so badly damaged that we cry out, "Oh, Lord, give me a high opinion of myself."

Recognizing Two Types of Self-Image

In terms of enduring patterns, we can identify two kinds of self-images: negative and positive. As we know, the negative self-image is by far the more common.

It is helpful to understand that we are created with three dimensions—physical, mental, and spiritual. These make up the whole person and provide the forms that reveal the self-image.

The negative self-image relative to the physical dimension is characterized by thoughts such as, "I'm ugly, unattractive, or physically unacceptable." Negative thoughts about the physical part of the person are as painful as they are numerous.

Other negative thoughts relate to the mental dimension. "I'm dumb, slow, or inferior" are thoughts that abound. "I have nothing of worth to contribute," such persons conclude. Another common characteristic of a person who has a negative self-image is that he compares other people's strengths with his own weaknesses. This results in many forms of personal loss. Poor choice of friends, low-paying jobs, or unnecessary mistreatment are just a few of the more commonly known. These unfortunate results can be especially tragic when the victim believes mistakenly that as a Christian, one must expect such mistreatment, failure, and disappointment because of a sense of humility.

The message is clear. Deep in human nature is the need for a person to feel that he is significant. When this need is frustrated, people suffer from hypersensitivity, envy, jealousy, arrogance, or shyness. In attempting to compensate for feelings of inferiority, people sometimes resort to alcohol, drugs, or illicit sex. In more extreme cases people turn to criminal behavior or even suicide.

But I believe that negative thoughts in the spiritual dimension can be the most serious. Such thoughts can be expressed as "I'm bad and don't deserve God's love" or "My life has no purpose." A sense of being alienated, alone, or cut off from our Creator is experienced. For these persons, life is meaningless. Hopelessness and despair inevitably invade their outlook.

In sharp contrast to the negative self-image, the positive self-image produces desirable effects. Physically, the person accepts his body, keeps it clean, exercises, eats sensibly, practices self-control, and gets enough rest and recreation.

Mentally, the person with the positive self-image believes that he is capable of setting and reaching realizable goals, making wise decisions, learning from mistakes, and solving problems of day-to-day living.

The spiritual evidences of positive self-image are a strong sense of purpose and an unwavering belief in God as a good God who causes all things to work together for the good of those who love him (Rom. 8:28). A prayerful attitude, a sense of being loved by God, and a desire to associate and worship with other believers are other benefits of a positive sense of self.

Biblical understanding of the nature of man explains why the problem of the negative self-image cannot be solved totally at the psychological level. More often than we realize, the diagnosis is found in the spiritual dimension.

Recently while watching an interview on television I saw evidence of how common the low self-image is among Christians. The wife of a well-known evangelist confessed that her self-image was so bad that she seriously entertained thoughts of suicide so that her husband could marry someone "better able to help him in his ministry."

While she spoke, the wife of the television host burst into tears and related how she, too, had struggled with feelings of inferiority that made her feel she was a hindrance to her husband's ministry.

Both couples then shared with their audience the spiritual battle they had fought. As a Christian counselor, I have witnessed this many times over the years and I am persuaded that most Christians do not understand the deceiving, accusing, condemning tactics of our common enemy, Satan. To be able to understand and overcome Satan's evil strategies we need to read very carefully and obey what Paul wrote in his letter to the Ephesians (6:10–17).

Satisfying the Need for Self-Esteem

The need for a sense of importance can be fulfilled in three ways. First, we can assert ourselves. Friedrich Nietzsche is often referred to as the leading prophet of self-assertion. He believed that "progress depends on the strong man and the strong people. Therefore be strong and assert yourself; be a superman."

Nietzsche sought to purge Christian thinking from civilized society. He attacked Christ's teaching with this paraphrase: "Ye have heard how it was said in old times, 'Blessed are the meek, for they shall inherit the earth'; but I say unto you, blessed are the valiant, for they shall make the earth their throne. And ye have heard men say, 'Blessed are the poor in spirit'; but I say unto you, blessed are the great in soul and the free in spirit, for they shall enter into Valhalla. And ye have heard men say, 'Blessed are the peacemakers'; but I say unto you, blessed are the war-makers, for they shall be called, if not the children of Yahiveh, the children of Odin, who is greater than Yahiveh."

Such thinking has led to terrorism, enslavement, and other expressions of "man's inhumanity to man." "Looking out for number one" and "doing it my way" are modern expressions of self-assertion that lead to disillusionment.

The second way of satisfying the hunger for self-esteem is the opposite of the first: self-negation. Those who believe in self-negation teach that one must stamp out the desire for self-importance. A cynical proponent of this position once stated, "Neither an egg nor an ego is any good until you break it." The two best-known religions that teach the elimination of desire are Hinduism and Buddhism.

According to Buddha, desire is the source of all evil and human suffering. He said, "You must free your soul of desire. Cut out the source of it. Denude your heart of every want, and in utterly passionless existence you will find peace of mind and contentment, and after much practice come at last to Nirvana, a state of nothingness."

Such teaching holds a certain fascination, even taking on the appearance of deep spirituality. But human instinct is given us by God and can never be eliminated by a religion of escape and negativism.

That brings us to the third answer, which is Christ's answer. Knowing what is in human nature, Christ rejected both self-assertion and self-negation. Instead he taught self-fulfillment. His way provides the only workable alternative to unrestrained satisfaction of our desires on the one hand and breaking the spirit on the other. When surrendered to Christ, the self with all its basically good desires becomes integrated, enriched, and fulfilled.

Developing a Positive Self-Image

The need for being able to place a high value on ourselves is best satisfied as we grow daily in Christian discipline, for Christ provides both a position and a pattern for self-appreciation. The position is "in Christ." Every believer has by faith been identified with Christ. In this greatest of all positions, we have infinite value because of Christ, his life, work, death, and resurrection. Once you realize this, you start building a great new self-image!

The pattern for solving the problem of how to value ourselves is in the way of Christ—walking with him, learning of him, and serving him. Self-esteem comes as a rich by-product of living this kind of pattern.

Self-image can be enriched by taking ten steps.

Believe that you can change your self-image. I recall a striking example of this point some years ago in a marriage-counseling case. The couple had separated before they came to see me. In talking with the husband, who initiated the separation, I learned that he left his wife because she was unable to express her feelings and didn't touch and caress enough. When I pointed this out to the wife, she replied, "Yes, I know, but I can't help it. That's just the way I am." (How many times do therapists hear that!)

"What you're telling me," I interpreted, "is that you have been the way you are for so long it seems natural?"

"Yes," she said. "Anything different would be unnatural for me."

I then reasoned with her. "Tell me, isn't your way of relating to your husband *learned?* You didn't inherit the way you show your feelings and express your affections, did you?"

She thought a minute and said, "Well, no, I guess not."

"That means your problem is the result of learning a pattern that is causing marital unhappiness. But that also means that you can be optimistic about changing because anything that is learned can be changed!"

"You mean that I can be more affectionate and love my husband the way he wants me to?" she asked.

"If you want to, you can!" I assured her.

Two weeks later the couple were together again. The husband could not believe the change in his wife. When I asked her how she managed all this she gave this insightful explanation: "When you told me that I could change, for the first time I believed that it *was* possible to change the way I was relating to my husband. After I believed I could do it, the rest just seemed to come along!"

When she changed her belief about herself and realized she could be more affectionate and more expressive, then her behavior changed.

Discover who you are. The search for and discovery of the self has never been more elegantly expressed than by Dietrich Bonhoeffer. Just before he was executed by the Nazis for his courageous participation in the German resistance movement, he penned the following:

Who Am I?

Who am I? They often tell me
I step from my cell's confinement
calmly, cheerfully, firmly,
like a squire from his country-house.
Who am I? They often tell me
I talk to my warders
freely and friendly and clearly,
as though it were mine to command.
Who am I? They also tell me
I bear the days of misfortune
equably, smilingly, proudly
like one accustomed to win.

Am I then really all that which other men tell of?
Or am I only what I know of myself,
restless and longing and sick, like a bird in a cage,

struggling for breath, as though hands were compressing
   my throat,
yearning for colours, for flowers, for the voices of birds,
thirsting for words of kindness, for neighborliness,
tossing in expectation of great events,
powerlessly trembling for friends at an infinite distance,
weary and empty at praying, at thinking, at making,
faint, and ready to say farewell to it all?

Who am I? This or the other?
Am I one person today, and tomorrow another?
Am I both at once? A hypocrite before others,
and before myself a contemptibly woebegone weakling?
or is something within me still like a beaten army,
fleeing in disorder from victory already achieved?
Who am I? They mock me, these lonely questions of
   mine.
Whoever I am, thou knowest, O God, I am thine!

As we have noted, most people are who they think
other people think they are. This is a great mistake.
Nothing does more to heighten self-consciousness, under-
mine self-confidence, and waste potential than too much
concern for "what others think." Successful people use a
more reliable, authoritative reference. They belong to the
positive, "abnormal" group!

Our reference for thinking about ourselves should be
what our great Creator thinks about us, not what other
people think. What we think he thinks should be learned
from sacred Scripture.

We are who the Bible says we are. David declared,
"When I consider thy heavens, the work of thy fingers,
the moon and the stars, which thou hast ordained; what
is man, that thou art mindful of him? and the son of
man, that thou visitest him?" (Ps. 8:3–4). When this passage is read, the emphasis should be placed on the excla-
mation *what is man!* The psalmist was awed by the great
contrast—the vast created universe on the one hand,
man on the other. Yet man receives the attention of God!

"What is man," he exclaims, "that thou art mindful of him." And he continues in the next verse: "For thou hast made him a little lower than the angels, and hast crowned him with glory and honour" (v. 5).

In these verses we are given a powerful prescription for overcoming the negative self-image. Imagine how special you are to receive such Divine attention!

When I counsel people regarding their self-image, I often use the example of Nehemiah, one of the heroes of the Old Testament. As he began to rebuild the wall of Jerusalem, his life was threatened. He was advised to escape. His reply gave impressive proof of the outworking of the self-image: "Should a man such as I flee?" (Neh. 6:11). His estimate of himself as the kind of man who would not take the coward's way out of danger gave him the courage to stay with the task that he eventually completed.

Feed your mind on positive, uplifting influences. As King Solomon wrote, "As [a man] thinketh in his heart, so is he" (Prov. 23:7). We are molding our self-image each day by the books we read, the tapes and music we listen to, and the people we associate with. Conscious effort to cultivate the positive influences will be richly rewarded.

Overcoming a negative self-image requires changing negative thoughts for positive thoughts. In this century, there have been three great contributions to this process of turning negative attitudes to positive attitudes.

In the early 1900s, William James said, "The greatest discovery of my generation is that human beings can alter their lives by altering their attitudes of mind."

Later, Maxwell Maltz wrote in *Psycho-Cybernetics*, "The most important psychological discovery of this century is the discovery of self-image."

More recently, Norman Vincent Peale has further developed the concept of positive mental attitude related to changing the self-image. By using the imagination positively, we can create mental images of what we would like to be. So powerful is this mental image that we can say, "The me I see is the me I'll be."

Robert Schuller used two Bible verses to break "the chain of inferiority feelings within [him]self":

Be confident in this one thing that God who has begun a good work in you [he has been giving you the will, the hope, the dream, the desire] will complete it! (Phil. 1:6).

For it is God working in you giving you the will and the power to achieve his purposes (Phil. 2:13).

Schuller interpreted these verses to mean that he would receive the secret, the strength, and the skill to succeed!

> If you think you are beaten, you are,
>   If you think you dare not, you don't,
> If you'd like to win, but you think you can't,
>   It's almost a cinch, you won't.
>
> If you think you'll lose, you've lost
>   For in the world we find
> Success begins with a fellow's will.
>   It's all in the state of mind.
>
> If you think you're outclassed, you are.
>   You've got to think high to rise.
> You've got to be sure of yourself before
>   You can ever win a prize.
>
> Life's battle doesn't always go
>   To the swifter or stronger man.
> But sooner or later the man who wins
>   Is the man who thinks he can.
>   —Anonymous

Counsel with qualified Christians who can help you gain insight into your problems. All of us from time to time need to benefit from the ministry of counseling. Such "privileged conversation" provides a nonthreatening climate that allows us to "exteriorize our [supposed] rottenness" when necessary, broaden our perspectives, clarify our choices, and identify our priorities. Such self-disclosure leads to greater self-acceptance and approval.

Learn that humility and self-confidence are not enemies. This balance has been expressed best by Paul: "I can do all things through Christ [who] strengthen[s] me" (Phil. 4:13). The belief that "I can do all things" (self-confidence) is linked with the qualifying phrase *through Christ*—that is, dependence on Christ and his resources (humility). This combination is unbeatable in developing a positive self-image.

A Methodist bishop, examining a class of ministerial students, asked them if they had a strong desire for great success in their chosen work. Not a one dared to admit such a desire, obviously afraid that such an admission would be interpreted as pride. Imagine their reaction when the bishop looked at the class and said, "Then you are a sorry lot, all of you."

Like many other people, those candidates for the ministry had failed to understand that a strong Christian ego can build humility with self-confidence and great appreciation. Satisfying the ego's need for importance does not necessarily lead to conceit, smugness, or using others to one's own advantage. As long as the self is surrendered to Christ, the normal, healthy ego's need for recognition and appreciation leads to a greater sense of well-being, personally richer relationships with others, and a much more productive pattern of living in general.

Start to live successfully today. Success builds a strong sense of self. You can plan your day so that you experience success. Begin by writing down your goals for the day. Each goal, no matter how insignificant, is important to reach. Your confidence will grow with each achievement. You will become more goal-oriented and you will feel more in control of your life. Successful days result in successful weeks; successful weeks result in successful months; and successful months result in successful years.

Build self-approval by building integrity. Self-approval and self-respect are permanently united. Without self-respect, we cannot possess a positive self-image, and self-respect is based on integrity. A person of integrity has the character to do what cannot be enforced—to love, to forgive, to resist temptation, and to choose life's highest and best.

This leads to self-respect, which A. Whitney Griswold reminds us cannot be hunted, purchased, or sold. "It comes to us when we are alone, in quiet moments, in quiet places, when we suddenly realize that knowing the good, we have done it, knowing the beautiful, we have served it, knowing the truth, we have done it."

Cultivate friendships that bring out your potential. Norman Vincent Peale tells an anecdote about Henry Ford, who once offered a visitor some advice that deserves to be cemented in our memory. "Son, you know something?" Ford asked, looking the man straight in the eyes. "And if you don't know it you had better find it out. You have a lot of potential in you. What you had better do is to associate with people who believe in you." Then he took a piece of paper and wrote, "Who is your best friend?" And here is Ford's remarkable answer: "Your best friend is he or she who helps you bring out of yourself the best that is in you."

Ideally these friendships should be formed with Christians in our churches. We are admonished by Paul to seek to excel in the building up of each other.

Cultivate the friendship of Christ. Ralph Waldo Emerson once wrote that our greatest search is for someone who can make us do what we can. The record of human history shows no one can compare with Jesus in his ability to change our lives. Friendship with him allows us the opportunity to become what we are capable of becoming.

> What a Friend we have in Jesus,
> All our sins and griefs to bear!
> What a privilege to carry
> Ev'rything to God in prayer.

A biblically defined relationship with God in Christ results in a conversion that is miraculous. "If any man be in Christ, he is a new creature: old things are passed away; behold, all things are become new" (2 Cor. 5:17). William James, perhaps the greatest student of human behavior in this century, studied the lives of men and women who had been converted. Based on his research, he defined conversion as "that process, gradual or sudden, by which a person hitherto divided, consciously wrong, inferior, and unhappy, becomes united, consciously right, superior, and happy."

Learn to love yourself. A wholesome self-love is essential to the development of a well-rounded personality. This kind of self-love is not associated with the illusion of perfection. It is a positive self-acceptance based on the knowledge that "if God loves me and accepts me in the finished work of Christ, then I am lovable and acceptable." Nothing can compare with an understanding of our position's privileges "in Christ" when it comes to building a positive self-image!

Charles L. Allen, former pastor of the First United Methodist Church in Houston, Texas, and a best-selling author, once told of a certain coed who did not know who her father was. Her personality lacked sparkle and her self-image obviously needed improving. Then one day, a wealthy, influential, impressive-looking man appeared on the campus and asked for her. He was her father! The transformation in the young woman was miraculous. When she realized who her father was, her self-image changed immediately from negative to positive!

In the family of God everybody is somebody special. As a certain celebrity said, "God made me and God don't make no junk." Our value to God is found in what Christ had done to save us. His life, death, resurrection, ascension, and intercession for us are revealed evidence of his love. And whenever a person is loved, he is important.

Overcoming the negative self-image can be accomplished by anyone who can say with conviction. "For I am sure that neither death, nor life, . . . nor anything else in all creation, will be able to separate [me] from the love of God in Christ Jesus [my] Lord" (Rom. 8:38–39, RSV).

A short time ago I witnessed the beauty and power of a discovery of self-worth in my wife, Mamie. In describing this experience to an audience in San Jose, California, she said, "All my life I felt I'd been encased in a thick covering of low self-image. My negative thoughts and feelings about myself caused me to withdraw socially because I felt that I couldn't be the person that others expected me to be. Then I discovered that I am special and that I can help others feel the same as I do. It was as though I'd been unzipped from my head to my toes and the real me stepped out. Now I am free!"

Making such a discovery often requires getting out of our "comfort zone," and that can be painful. As my wife explained, "The zipper is controlled from the inside. Only you can make the decision to release yourself. If you don't make it, you hurt. If you do make it, you hurt. Either way there is pain. But the pain of unzipping is temporary and the pain of remaining locked up within yourself can last a lifetime."

As one of the world's spiritual and intellectual giants wrote, "We are God's work of art, created in Christ Jesus to live the good life as from the beginning he had meant for us to live it" (Eph. 2:10, author's paraphrase). When we know who we are (God's work of art) and what our purpose and privilege is (created in Christ Jesus to live the good life as from the beginning he had meant for us to live it) we have the answer to the old Scotsman's (and your and my) prayer: "Oh, Lord, give me a high opinion of myself."

6

Conquering Boredom, Depression, and Spiritual Sickness

When Ted sat down heavily in my consulting room, he shook his head, managed a weak grin, and said, "I don't understand it."

I waited for him to continue.

"My life has bogged down. Nothing seems to interest me. I don't have any energy; I'm tired all the time. I feel more like a robot than a person. I'm just going through the motions without any emotions. Inside me is a desert."

"Have you had a thorough physical examination lately?" I asked.

"Yes," Ted replied, "that's why I'm here. The doctor couldn't find anything wrong with me physically."

"Before I became a Christian," he continued, "these feelings wouldn't have bothered me nearly as much as they do now." Then he paused, and with a pained expression on his face, said, "A Christian isn't supposed to feel this way, is he?"

I assured Ted that he had accurately described a condition which sooner or later most of us experience. It can take several forms, ranging from the blahs to boredom or even depression when it becomes severe. Sometimes it takes the form of spiritual slackness. It's been creatively called "the common cold of the psyche," "November in the soul," and "the black night of the soul."

Students of the Old Testament know that this emotional low tide is not a new problem. Consider these quotes from long ago:

I am weary of my life (Gen. 27:46).

Why are thou cast down, O my soul? and why art thou disquieted within me? (Ps. 43:5).

Therefore is my spirit overwhelmed within me; my heart within me is desolate (Ps. 143:4).

Perhaps the most reported symptom of this emotional condition is fatigue. A survey by the National Ambulatory Medical Care Association found that fatigue is the seventh most frequent reason why people go to the doctor. In 1975, there were 10.5 million visits by people complaining of listlessness, tiredness, or weariness, described by the medical term *lassitude*. And these patients represent only a small percentage of those who actually have these symptoms.

What's wrong with people who are "sick and tired"? The problem is not easily solved because it has a wide variety of causes—physical, psychological, and spiritual (which are not even recognized by most authorities), and it resists therapy.

In one study, for example, 39 percent of the reported problems were physical, 41 percent were psychological, 12 percent were mixed, and 8 percent were undetermined.

The best known psychological causes for lassitude include depression, grief, chronic anxiety, stress resulting from life changes, insomnia, and boredom.

In our country mental-health specialists now say boredom and depression are their clients' most common symptoms. Actually, boredom is an international problem. The Romans called it *taedium* and the French call it ennui.

Among our modern writers, T. S. Eliot is often cited for his ability to express this feeling of stagnation and emptiness. As one of his characters, Prufrock, says,

I have known them all already,
known them all.
Have known the evenings, mornings, afternoons,
I have measured out my life with coffee spoons.

Some time ago a bus driver in New York City startled his passengers by announcing, "Twenty years I've been driving this route and see that light? For twenty years I've been turning left at that light, but *this* time I'm turning right! 'Cause I'm going to Miami! If you don't want to go, get off now." Seventeen people stayed on the bus and went to Miami with him. When they returned, reporters asked them why they went. They explained, "We were sick and tired of being sick and tired."

We have little trouble explaining why those who cut themselves off from the source of life experience emptiness or soul sickness. What we are rarely prepared for, as Christians, is when our own soul seems dry as a desert and as lifeless as a tomb. However, we can be thankful that Scripture and Christian autobiography and biography down through church history give reassuring witness to the fact that this arid condition is much more common than many think.

Often referred to as the "black night of the soul," this spiritual slackness has afflicted such godly people as Albert Schweitzer, Martin Luther, and Theresa of Ávila. Old Testament giants such as Isaiah, Jeremiah, and the psalmist David were not exempt. Neither are you and I.

Honesty and openness among long-time Christians reveal that at times, in spite of our church attendance, prayers, Bible study, and all that normally is associated with Christian behavior, we "feel" alone, deserted, forsaken by God. All our best efforts to regain our zest for living seem futile.

This distressing condition is made even more painful by the fear, guilt, confusion, and despair that accompany it. Questions torment us: "Have I caused God to turn his back upon me?" "What would others think if they knew how I'm really feeling?" "What does this mean?" "How long will this last?" "Is this the way a true Christian feels?"

Usually these doubts are kept secret. This increases the burden. Even worse is the effect of attempting to deceive ourselves and others, pretending that nothing is wrong and that we're enjoying what no normal Christian can possibly enjoy.

Toward Greater Self-Understanding

To be able to accurately diagnose the problem is to take a giant step toward cure. As we have already seen, the negative emotional condition we are dealing with in this chapter is complex. Fatigue, boredom, depression, spiritual slackness—all these are interrelated. I hope the topics are covered in such a way as to help the reader increase his understanding and take appropriate action. In this way immediate movement in the direction of better living can begin.

A good beginning can be made in increasing our understanding by carefully studying the following check list:

1. simple fatigue (My life's out of balance with an overemphasis on work.)
2. dietary deficiency (I'm not getting the proper nourishment necessary for good health.)
3. lack of stimulation or excitement (I wonder, Is this all there is?)
4. leisure time (I've too much time on my hands.)
5. emotional constipation (I cannot express my feelings.)
6. emotional insulation (I refuse to feel because it hurts too much.)
7. avoidance (If I don't think about it, maybe it will go away.)

8. conflict (Part of me says, I ought to . . . and part of me says, But I'd rather. . . .)
9. fear (I'm afraid to desire anything.)
10. guilt (My conscience confines me.)
11. grief (I've suffered a great loss.)
12. lack of goals (I don't know what to do.)
13. absence of purpose (My life is not going anywhere that is really important.)
14. absence of meaning (Life is meaningless.)

Negative Emotions Can Have Positive Meanings

Although the fourteen items in the list were negative, negative emotions can have positive meaning. Keen students of developmental psychology have observed that boredom, for example, is a necessary part of the passage from one stage of life to another. About every ten years we enter a new stage of development. The transition is characterized by two movements: letting go of what is no longer appropriate and taking on what is needed for the new stage. To some writers this amounts to a death and rebirth. Old enthusiasms and interests fade and new ones take their place—and boredom follows that normal reduction of excitement that can actually be leading to opportunity for more meaningful, joyful, and productive beginnings.

Most of my clients needing help with boredom have been middle-aged. Why should boredom grip those entering their midthirties, the chronological onset of middle age? These middle years have been strikingly described as a span of life during which people are "too young to fail and yet too old to succeed." The meaning of this statement is understood by studying the pattern of surprisingly large numbers of people. Their beginning is often impressive. Motivated by high ideals of youth, they work hard, achieving one goal after another. Gradually, however, often without being recognized, dreams fade, strength wanes, and the pace slackens. A growing sense of "what's it all about" is like an emotional termite eating away the structure of their inner lives.

Actually the essence of the person is being revealed, making possible a higher degree of self-discovery than has previously been experienced. During this passage persons with enough insight and courage are learning to accept themselves more completely. They are shedding layer after layer of imposed expectations and beliefs. They have learned—usually through disappointment, failure, and disillusionment—what does not work for them, where they do not fit, and what they are not able to do. Rather than try to persist in living with psychological and spiritual burdens that frustrate, confuse, and misdirect, they are allowing "the real self to stand up." This process is healthy and even vital if the next stage of life is to be really lived. With such significant changes taking place, it is no wonder that the emotional part of the struggling self seeks shelter in a state of boredom, depression, or spiritual emptiness.

Another positive meaning of fatigue, boredom, and spiritual slackness is this: It can be a prelude to a higher level of living where you feel more at home in the spiritual kingdom. Such was the experience of C. H. Spurgeon, one of the greatest preachers England ever produced. Here is his own remarkable testimony:

> Before any great achievement, some measure of depression is very usual. . . . Such was my experience when I first became a pastor in London. My success appalled me, and the thought of the career which seemed to open up, so far from elating me, cast me into the lowest depth, out of which I uttered my miserere and found no room for a gloria in excelsis. Who was I that I should continue to lead so great a multitude? I would betake me to my village obscurity, or emigrate to America and find a solitary nest in the backwoods where I might be sufficient for the things that were demanded of me. It was just then the

curtain was rising on my lifework, . . . This depression comes over me whenever the Lord is preparing a larger blessing for my ministry.*

Negative emotions often signal the soul's sighing from its aspiration but being stuck in the rut of a pattern of living made burdensome by sins, mistakes, noble resolutions unkept, and acceptance of other people's negative evaluations. Failures, disappointments, losses, or frustrations become barnacles of the soul, weighing it down and making its progress seem increasingly difficult. These signals can provide insight into our nature as human beings. For as one author wrote, "And here at last we find strict diagnosis of our malady, which is in short, that man is heaven-starved. Men are born thirsty for infinity."

Phillips Brooks reminds us that "the ideal life is in our blood and never will be still. Sad will be the day for any man when he becomes contented with the thoughts he is thinking and the deeds he is doing—where there is not forever beating at the doors of his soul some great desire to do something larger, which he knows that he was meant and made to do." And so we can reasonably come to share Ralph Waldo Emerson's belief that "our chief want in life is somebody who can make us do what we can."

Fascinating research continues to shed light on the study of human potential. A group of psychiatrists has been studying the brain tissue of cadavers for many years. This research is being carried out to determine the extent to which these people activated their brain cells during their lifetime. Their startling finding? The average person activated approximately 7 to 8 percent of his total brain cells in his lifetime. The geniuses such as those on the level of an Albert Einstein activated only about 10 to 12 percent of their brain cells during their lifetimes.

*Quoted in Charles R. Swindoll, *Hand Me Another Brick* (Nashville: Thomas Nelson, 1978), p. 88.

Such findings agree with the conclusion reached by the American Psychiatric Association. After several years of studying the causes of fatigue in today's world, and especially in the United States, researchers concluded that the primary cause of fatigue in the lives of most people is the failure to have something to live for that seems bigger and more important than themselves.

Careful readers of the Bible recall the words of Jesus, who warned his listeners of the effect of self-centered living. He said, "Whoever finds his life will lose it, and whoever loses his life for my sake will find it" (Matt. 10:39, NIV).

In the Middle Ages the church drew up a list of the seven deadly sins—pride, envy, anger, sloth, covetousness, gluttony, and lust. For our purpose let's pay particular attention to sloth or accidie, defined as "that dull state of soul where nothing has any meaning and no action is worth taking." This unflattering condition is called a sin because it is willfully allowed.

There is a self-dramatizing effect produced by this subtle sin. "Look at how unhappy, miserable, and weak I am" is the message that the accidie-infected personality sends to the world. This sin is not only filled with self-pity but also quickly gains strength every time it is yielded to. What it seeks is sympathy but what it needs is something quite different.

A person who gives in to accidie can be accurately described as a bore—"someone who deprives you of solitude without providing you with company." He leaves you with a feeling that you have clouds over your head and weights on your feet.

Elsie Robinson was not exaggerating when she said, "Unpleasantness can be a disease. It provides an escape for our cowardice, an excuse for our laziness, an alibi for our cussedness, and a spotlight for our conceit."

Our generation is familiar with such expressions as "looking out for number one," "I did it my way," or "winning by intimidation." This has been aptly described as "the tedious egotism of our day." The result? A self that is constantly burdened by its own self-centeredness. Selfish living is self-defeating, as David, reporting Israel's rebellion, reminds us: "He gave them their request; but sent leanness into their soul" (Ps. 106:15). And Jeremiah wrote of those who "went after empty idols and became empty themselves" (Jer. 2:5, *Moffatt*).

Fatigue, boredom, burnout, and depression can sometimes be explained in light of what we know about phases of adventure. Paul Tournier, a noted Swiss therapist, has clearly shown the nature and development of any new endeavor that begins as an adventure.

Tournier believes that peculiar to man is the "great impulse toward adventure" which he considers to be an instinct. In *The Adventure of Living*, he shows how every adventure follows the same pattern and can be described by the same curve. First there is an abrupt ascent, explosive, spontaneous, contagious. Then the joy of discovery becomes reduced to organization and standardization. What was new and exciting now is routine and dreary. "Adventure ceases," writes Tournier, "as soon as normalcy begins." Thus the need for renewal continues throughout life.

Tournier makes an important distinction between quality adventure and quantity adventure. The quality adventure is the reach of the spirit for realization of the ultimate experience of value, of quality. The quantity adventure is a compensation for failure to satisfy the soul's quest for God. This shift in adventure leads to a vicious circle. Money and things become the prize for the person on a quantity adventure. But enough is always a little more than what he has. And so the more quantity is sought the less it satisfies, and the dissatisfaction increases the quest for more. "Life consisteth not in the abundance of things which [a man] possesseth" (Luke 12:15).

Someone has well said that "the tragedy of life is not in the fact of death itself. The tragedy of life is in what dies inside a man while he lives—the death of genuine feeling, the death of inspired response, the death of the awareness that makes it possible to feel in oneself the pain in the glory of other men."

William James reminds us that whatever is worth possessing must be paid for in daily installments of effort. All of us desire the expanding life. We shrink back from the picture of ourselves growing in years but deteriorating in spirit. We think, "I will keep my mind young and active by reading good books, by cultivating finer tastes in art and music, by nourishing my spirit through worship and meditation." But these worthy intentions are not self-sustaining. Postponement can lay its frosty hand upon them and they can shrivel and die. "By neglecting the necessary concrete labor, by sparing ourselves the little daily tax," James warns, "we are positively digging the graves of our higher possibilities."

How quickly the adventurous mind can become the set mind. Nobody wants to be identified with the person whose mind was said to be like cement—thoroughly mixed and permanently set! James shocked the teachers who heard him say, "Old fogyism begins at a younger age than we think. I am almost afraid to say so, but I believe that in the majority of human beings it begins at about twenty-five." James's judgment, made several generations ago, was recently validated by a United Press survey. The "typical American" is twenty-seven years old and reads less than one book a year. His values are primarily materialistic. He is satisfied with trivial pleasures and is bored with theological matters. He may attend church twenty-seven times a year, but he is indifferent toward the supernatural and spends little time thinking about life after death. Instead of being interested in immortality he absorbs himself principally with football, fishing, and mechanics. Thus the "typical American" evidently finds himself experiencing the following:

> O God! O God!
> How weary, stale, flat, and unprofitable
> Seem to be all the uses of this world.
> Fie on it! Ah fie! 'Tis an unweeded garden
> That grows to seed.
> —*Hamlet* (I. ii. 129)

Undisciplined living leads to dead ends, as Ralph Barton, a popular cartoonist, discovered. When he took his own life, he left behind this message: "I have run from wife to wife, from house to house, and from country to country in a ridiculous effort to escape from myself. In doing so, I am very much afraid I have caused a great deal of unhappiness to those who have loved me. . . . No one is responsible for this . . . except myself. I've done it because I'm fed up with inventing devices for getting through twenty-four hours every day."

On New Year's Day some years ago an eighteen-year-old left this suicide note:

Nothing happened last year to make life worthwhile. A year ago exactly I made a sort of bargain with God or fate, and this is my part of the bargain. I agreed if something didn't happen last year to make life worth living and to make me somebody, that at the end of the year, I would quit living. That wasn't asking too much, but I didn't get it. Please don't think this is something brought on by late events. . . . I just don't have the courage to go on living.

Often people suffering from boredom are trying to *find* life worth living. Such an expectation is doomed to failure. Nobody finds life worth living. We must learn to *make* life worth living. Life is a mirror reflecting what we bring to it. If we are empty, negative, and self-centered then that is what life reflects.

Our Most Difficult Emotional Experience

The most difficult experience that Christians have is feeling forsaken or abandoned by God. One who experienced this loss of a sense of God's presence was a highly regarded English minister and author named L. Austin Sparks. In one of his books, *His Great Love,* he describes spiritual growth as progressing in stages. To continue to grow in our understanding of Christ, the church, and the deeper meaning of being identified with Christ, Sparks believes that "something has to happen to us, get down to the bottom and clean out all that has gone before us." He adds, "We go through a new experience of death and desolation and emptiness, of hopelessness, in order to come to something further as in the divine revelation."

There is no agony like this agony of the soul that has grown to thrive on the communion with the indwelling Christ but now has lost touch with that precious life-giving source. "It is not a wrong thing to say," Sparks writes, "when the Lord hides himself, when the Lord lets us feel that we are left alone, when the Lord seems to close the heavens to us so that there is not to-and-fro communication. Everything that we had looked for, expected and preached, seems to have come to an end and to have broken down, and we are just left in what seems like the ruin of everything."

Such experiences, baffling and painful as they may be, have a purpose. Again Sparks explains, "People who are going to count for Him go through deep experiences like that, and the object is to get them on to a basis which will make it possible for Him to use them."

Our future usefulness then will depend upon our response to this agonizing sense of spiritual abandonment. During these difficult times, the anchor that holds is not our emotions, but faith that obeys, in spite of feeling. "Lovest thou me?" asks the Lord. Before we glibly answer yes, we should heed Sparks's reminder: "Only

God knows, how difficult it is—to love Him for Himself when He does not seem to be doing anything for us at all. That is the challenge of love."

Climbing Out of the Emotional Basement

Because the emotional conditions described in this chapter are characterized by absence of strong desire, popular off-the-cuff solutions are usually ineffective. It's easy enough to advise, "Do something exciting," "Find a new stimulating interest," "Take a Caribbean cruise," or "Go get a checkup." When the will to do has atrophied, miring the person in deep emotional ruts, any suggestion that requires expending energy usually fails.

1. That is why "getting off dead center" requires us first to learn to become great receivers. When we become receptive—open, hospitable, hungry, inviting—we immediately create the possibility of replenishing our resources or developing new resources, or both. By quietly and prayerfully meditating on Christ and sacred Scripture, we can receive new energy and new motivation. "But as many as received him, to them gave he power to become the sons of God" (John 1:12).

We cannot give out what we have not taken in. Life's rhythm requires learning to take in, to receive as well as to act and do. All too often in our achievement-oriented society, we lose sight of the fundamental importance of the first stage in rich, rhythmic living, the stage of receiving. Many times I have said to my clients, "Stop trying so hard and relax. Learn to be a great receiver." Begin each new day by opening your mind and heart to Christ, receiving his love, wisdom, forgiveness, peace, and power. Meditate prayerfully and thoughtfully on two of my favorite verses: "My God shall supply all your need according to his riches in glory by Christ Jesus" (Phil. 4:19) and "They that wait upon the LORD shall renew their strength" (Isa. 40:31).

2. Meditate on the sufferings of Christ. Nothing has the power to stir, energize, and stimulate the soul like gazing on the figure of Christ hanging on the cross. Charges of morbidity notwithstanding, the person who allows himself to think deeply on the passion and death of Jesus will find himself shaken out of his lethargy and complacency. There is no cure like Calvary for our being unprofitable because of the way we feel.

3. Go from Calvary to Pentecost. The crucified Savior rose again! After his ascension some 120 of his followers gathered in the upper room in Jerusalem and received their baptism in the Holy Spirit. They were given Pentecostal power for a Pentecostal task, that being to evangelize the world.

4. Paul counsels, "Have your mind renewed, and so be transformed in nature, able to make out what the will of God is" (Rom. 12:2, *Moffatt*). The renewed mind—that is the answer! And when is the mind renewed? When it is "able to make out what the will of God is." Our nature is transformed by linking our mind with the will of God. When the mind functions in harmony with the heart, where life's deepest preferences are, and the will of God is desired and discerned, resources for abundant living are released.

5. More often than not, our emotions need use, not more rest. But emotional expressions must take forms that are useful to others, satisfying to ourselves, and pleasing to Christ.

Our churches are full of people rushing here and there doing good deeds but feeling inwardly miserable. They are so ego-involved in their service that what means most to them is applause, recognition, and gratitude. Naturally such persons suffer deep disappointment because their expectations are unrealistic. They often end up in the pastor's study disillusioned, weary, and confused.

Our emotions are highly charged with energy and

must find healthy means of expression. If this does not happen, the emotions turn inward. Blocked by inactivity, suppression, and excessive self-concern, the emotional life stagnates, sickens, and causes fatigue, boredom, depression, even physical sickness. Ingrown emotions are worse than ingrown toenails! This is why James counsels, "Never . . . suffer one's self to have an emotion . . . without expressing it afterward in *some* active way. Let the expression be the least thing in the world—speaking generally to one's grandmother, or giving up one's seat in a horse-carriage, if nothing more heroic—but let it not fail to take place."

Negative emotions produced by procrastination, blaming others, and excusing ourselves can be changed by positive actions of obedience to God's Word.

6. Another energizing influence is the ability to positively encounter life's difficulties and challenges. The late Lillian Gilbreth lived a remarkable life. Some of the highlights, which are preserved in the book and movie *Cheaper by the Dozen,* are instructive:

> She was left with twelve children to rear when her husband died. Not only did she keep her family together, but also she saw to it that each child completed his education.
>
> She took control of the small consulting business her husband started and made it highly successful.
>
> She was named outstanding management thinker in the world and awarded a medal for this in Czechoslovakia.
>
> She had more honorary degrees conferred upon her than did any president of the United States.
>
> She was voted this nation's Mother of the Year.
>
> She published numerous papers and books on the subject of time and motion study and related areas of work efficiency.

When asked the secret of her success, Gilbreth replied, "I'll be happy to tell you. My secret is that every morning I ask the Lord to provide me with some new obstacles and difficulties."

"Is that it?" responded the disappointed interviewer.

"No," she said, "there's more. Every night I always *thank* him because he always answers my morning prayer."

"Dr. Gilbreth, you've already told me you're eighty-seven. When do you think you'll reach an age when you'll no longer ask the Lord for obstacles and difficulties?"

She smiled and said, "Young man, come around and ask me that when I reach middle age."

As the interview continued, she shared a more detailed explanation of her brief, provocative remarks. She frankly admitted that when her husband died, she had moments of despair. But with twelve children depending upon her, she made the decision to make a success of the consulting firm and slowly built it to a profitable level. "Somewhere along the way," she reflected, "I began to realize, as a result of the research I'd carried out, the exciting life that Frank and I had had together, and other factors, that boredom and lack of challenge were the chief enemies of a long, happy, and productive life."

Her experience gradually led to a bold practice of actually "seeking out challenges and tough situations to research and solve." Such an aggressive approach led to this insight: "I came to realize more and more that those were the moments in which I truly felt totally alive, creative, healthy and happy." She began to notice as the years went by how many of her friends and colleagues lost their health and productive ability in direct proportion to the extent to which they avoided challenging situations. "Many of them," she observed sadly, "played it safe and secure and just lost their basic zest for living."

Several decades ago one of the leading thinkers in human behavior was a noted psychologist, writer, and researcher, Henry C. Link. He was asked by a well-funded foundation to find the main reason for happiness in the United States. He carefully chose a group of prominent researchers from related disciplines. Then they carefully selected a cross section of people and began their investigation. These scholars analyzed the meaning of happiness and finally reached a unanimous agreement regarding its definition.

At the end of a year, the committee members announced they were ready to release a one-thousand-page report to the press. When the reporters met with Link and his associates, they asked for a statement that would summarize the massive research. This is the famous summary that Link gave: *Virtually every day of his life the happy American does, or attempts to do, something difficult.*

Abraham Lincoln attended church on Sunday and listened to a sermon that many thought was inspired by the pastor's knowledge that the president of the United States was in his congregation. When someone asked what he thought of the sermon, President Lincoln said, "Since you've asked, I must confess, I didn't think much of it."

"Why?" asked the inquirer.

Lincoln explained, "Because he didn't ask us to do anything great."

7. Develop the servant mentality and give yourself to some cause in the kingdom of God. Modern psychology is finding out what the Old Testament sage knew years ago: "Where there is no vision, the people perish" (Prov. 29:18). Great dreams and purposes, challenging causes and programs have an elevating, energizing effect on personality. John Wanamaker, the great merchant, shared this insight: "The most important lesson I have learned is that I have the least trouble with myself when I am giving myself to a worthwhile cause."

"Tell me how to live happily with myself," a girl asked

Alice Freeman Palmer at a vacation school in the Boston slums. She answered, "Do something for somebody every day!"

"I have a cure for boredom that never will fail," said one woman with a reputation for usefulness. "It is made up of ten rules. Go out among the people and perform one kind act ten times."

8. Furthermore, we can experience more zest for life by developing better balance in our lives.

The Mayo clinic at Rochester, Minnesota, tested people who were chronically tired. They found that their fatigue did not result from expenditure of energy but from living an unbalanced life. Using Dr. Richard Clarke Cabot's formula of work, play, love, and worship, the Mayo Clinic made a cross of four arms of equal length to represent the balanced life. "When one or more are stubs, the result is unhappiness, a frequent forerunner of fatigue. Thus a businessman's cross may have overlong work and love arms and stubby play and worship arms; a debutante is long on play and short on work; a spinster may be long on work and worship but short on love and play."

9. Also, we need to learn to love life through labor. Kahlil Gibran, the Syrian poet and philosopher, had an unusual grasp of this point. He wrote, "Always you have been told that work is a curse and labor is a misfortune. But I say to you that when you work you fulfill a part of earth's furthest dream, assigned to you when that dream was born, and in keeping yourself in labor you are in truth loving life. And to love life through labor is to be intimate with life's inmost secret." Consider also the words of John Wesley: "Never be unemployed and never be triflingly employed."

10. Grow something—a flower, a shrub, a vegetable, a tree. Visit a nursery; read magazine articles on how to grow what you would like to plant. Getting involved in preparing, planting, cultivating, and enjoying the results of your efforts can be a great tonic. In addition, lessons

relating to the partnership between God and man are revealed to the gardener.

11. Develop a faith that courageously encounters the real world. Tournier wrote in *The Adventure of Living*, "Faith, far from turning us away from the world, brings us back to it. . . . It awakens in us a new interest in the world, in the concrete reality of every day, hard, laborious, difficult, often painful as it is, but wonderful nevertheless. The joy of living, of making an effort, of having a goal to aim at, the joy of moving a finger, smelling a perfume, of looking at something, of hearing a voice, of learning something and loving someone."

12. The "attitude of gratitude" is a great lift for the sinking spirit. Gratitude focuses on the blessings and benefits we already have and the loving source from which they came, and radically improves our perspective. The grateful person attracts help, opportunity, and positive responses from others. Gloom and depression cannot co-exist with gratitude. So, in the words of the familiar refrain,

> Count your blessings,
> Name them one by one;
> Count your many blessings,
> See what God has done.

13. Be unsparing in searching out any self-pity. Follow Muriel Lester's advice: "Hunt for self-pity as you would hunt for lice." "And loathe it," adds E. Stanley Jones, "with the same loathing."

14. One of the most beneficial things we can do to help ourselves out of the doldrums is to get outdoors and experience some of nature's therapy. There came a time in Emerson's life when his spirit sagged and he plummeted to his own emotional cellar. He was counseled by a wise old aunt to get out of doors and allow the world of nature to speak to him of larger things. He followed her advice and experienced the healing power of nature.

Immanuel Kant, the philosopher, said, "Two things fill me with unutterable awe, the stars above me, and the moral law within me." Thousands of years before Kant, the psalmist exclaimed,

The heavens are telling the glory of God;
    and the firmament proclaims his handiwork (Ps. 19:1,
    RSV).

Read the four Gospels and notice how much time Jesus spent outdoors and how he spoke of birds and lilies.

15. Use the "as-if" principle. Years ago, James taught this: "If you want a quality, act as if you already had it."

In *How I Raised Myself from Failure to Success in Selling,* Frank Bettger tells how he learned the importance of the "as-if" principle. As a young man, Bettger wanted to be a professional baseball player. He started with a minor-league team but was let go because of lack of enthusiasm.

He signed with another team at a lower salary and continued to play without zest. Then one day, a famous retired professional said to him, "Frank, don't you really like baseball? You have real ability, but you are totally lacking in enthusiasm, and until you get that you will never go ahead in this sport, or for that matter, in anything else in life. You must have enthusiasm. It's a primary requisite for success."

Predictably, Bettger protested, "But what can I do? I haven't got enthusiasm. You just can't go out and buy it in a store. You either have it or you don't. I haven't, so that's it, I guess."

"You're wrong, Frank," replied the wise old pro. "Make yourself act enthusiastic. It's as simple as that. Act with enthusiasm, play ball with enthusiasm, and pretty soon you will have enthusiasm. Once you're fired with conviction, your natural talents will take you to the top . . . ."

It was the great turning point in Bettger's life. By acting

"as if" he had enthusiasm, he actually developed it and soon rose to the major leagues. When an injury forced him to leave baseball, he became an insurance salesman. Once again he was infected with apathy. This time, however, he reminded himself of what he had learned about the "as-if" principle. In a short time, he overcame his indifference and rose to the top in his career.

16. If the boredom remains, or deepens into depression that stubbornly persists, you should consult a qualified Christian counselor (see chapter 9). Gustave Flaubert believed that "the most glorious moments in life are not the so-called days of success, but rather those days when out of dejection and despair you feel in you a challenge to life, and the promise of future accomplishments."

> Breathe on me, Breath of God,
>   Fill me with life anew,
> That I may love what Thou dost love,
>   And do what Thou wouldst do.
>
> Breathe on me, Breath of God.
>   Till I am wholly Thine,
> Till all this earthly part of me
>   Glows with Thy fire divine.

Jonah experienced such a turning point. He stated, "When my soul fainted within me I remembered the LORD" (Jonah 2:7). We can be renewed, energized, and made productive by following the rebellious prophet's example: "I remembered the Lord." Obedience to his word will then lead to putting on "the garment of praise for the spirit of heaviness" (Isa. 61:3).

J. B. Phillips, best known for his translation of the New Testament, *The New Testament in Modern English,* engaged in a lifelong battle with anxiety and depression. The following words from his personal correspondence will be greatly encouraging to others who are experiencing spiritual and mental struggle:

These periods of spiritual dryness which every saint has known are the very times when your need of God is greatest. To worship him may or may not bring back the lost 'feeling', but your contact with God in prayer and praise will strengthen you spiritually, whether you feel it or not. . . . Times of spiritual apathy are the very times when we can do most to prove our love for God, and I have no doubt we bring most joy to his heart when we defy our feelings and act in spite of them.

If you give in to your 'feelings' you tend to become their slave, whether it is in the religious sphere or any other, and in any case you remain shockingly immature. The mature Christian gains his maturity largely by the exercise of his faith, and that means continuing to believe in God in spite of appearances and in spite of feelings. Give in to your feelings and you fall back; defy them and you may win a thrilling victory . . . and even if you don't, you have taken another step towards maturity.

What we need is continued courage and faith. If we are angry with God I'm sure he doesn't mind! To go on believing without knowing is what faith is all about. I will only say, don't lose your basic faith however much it is superficially scarred and pitted by this temporary life.

It is not so much our desperate attempts to hang on to God as God's unfailing will to 'keep us' that is so important.

As far as you can, and God knows how difficult this is, try to relax in and upon him. As far as my experience goes, to get even a breath of God's peace in the midst of pain is infinitely worth having.

It is much more than a crumb of comfort to know that whatever we feel, God knows all about it. Even when we find it next to impossible to pray, I am basically convinced that he understands this too.

I have been through prolonged periods of utter darkness and a good deal of mental pain and have by the grace of God won through.*

*Quoted in Vera Phillips and Edwin Robertson, *J. B. Phillips, the Wounded Healer* (Grand Rapids: Eerdmans, 1984), pp. 109–10.

7

Facing Suffering

I've got so many problems I hardly know where to begin," sighed my client. We all know that feeling. Few of us live very long before some unpredictable, undesirable experience comes our way. In spite of our best efforts to avoid these painful experiences, we all learn first-hand the truth of the ancient insight: "Man is born to trouble as the sparks fly upward" (Job 5:7).

As a Christian psychotherapist, I have spent many years confronting the problems of suffering. Into my consulting room walk people who are hurting—children, adolescents, young adults, middle-aged people, and the elderly. No human being is exempt from pain.

Early in my counseling experience I began to realize that an adequate life philosophy must include a way of coping with adversity. But where is this "way"? And how do we find it? And once it is found, how do we walk in it?

These sobering questions puzzled me as I attended the university. And though my search led to the acknowledged authorities in the fields of mental health, philosophy, and religion, I became convinced that the most authoritative and reliable help was not found in the textbooks and journals (though I appreciated the insights I often found in them).

Both my training and experience persuaded me that a biblically-defined relationship to God as revealed in Jesus Christ is our most reliable source of understanding and means of overcoming life's difficulties. The Bible is the book that reveals the deepest truth about human nature and about the right choices to make in life. As the psalmist said, "Thy word is a lamp unto my feet and a light unto my pathway" (Ps. 119:105). This insight is forever contemporary, and so the Bible is my most treasured reference book.

The wisest man in the world of his day, King Solomon, wrote: "In the day of prosperity be joyful, but in the day of adversity consider" (Eccles. 7:14). If we are wise, then, we must give careful thought "in the day of adversity" to *consider*.

The Storms of Life

A good place to begin our considerations is Christ's Sermon on the Mount (Matt. 7:24–29). This passage has special meaning for suffering people and ought to be required reading for all of us. Christ concluded his sermon with a parable which is commonly known as "the parable of the two foundations":

> Therefore whosoever heareth these sayings of mine, and doeth them, I will liken him unto a wise man, which built his house upon a rock:
> And the rain descended, and the floods came, and the winds blew, and beat upon that house; and it fell not: for it was founded upon a rock.
> And every one that heareth these sayings of mine, and doeth them not, shall be likened unto a foolish man, which built his house upon the sand:
> And the rain descended, and the floods came, and the winds blew, and beat upon that house; and it fell: and great was the fall of it.
> And it came to pass, when Jesus had ended these sayings, the people were astonished at his doctrine:
> For he taught them as one having authority, and not as the scribes.

Christ's listeners recognized that his words rang true; they conveyed realism, undiluted and straight from the shoulder. The first point made clear in the parable is that the *storms are a part of life*. We are not told what *kind* of trouble Christ was describing. Life's storms can take many forms. We can suffer physical pain and illness, mental and emotional disturbance, and spiritual distress.

The second point that comes through in the parable is the most shocking of all. Christ tells of a storm that hit the house of the person who was living a good life. He was described as a wise man who heard and obeyed the teachings of Scriptures. So why did he have to suffer?

Later on Jesus declared, "Here on earth you will have many trials and sorrows" (John 16:33, LB). In 1 Peter 4:12 we read: "Dear friends, don't be bewildered or surprised when you go through the fiery trials ahead, for this is no strange, unusual thing that is going to happen to you" (LB). Most people find this idea difficult to accept. We can understand *deserved* suffering, but *undeserved* suffering—that baffles the wisest among us.

Sue's problem is an example of what we are considering. Her second child, less than a year old, had been born with a physical handicap that required hospital treatments twice each week. The financial and emotional strains were mounting, and Sue had twice tried to take her own life. She came to my office in a desperate effort to get help.

"I just don't understand it," she cried. "I've been a Christian since I was a little girl. My husband and I have been faithful to church. We pay our tithes and we pray each day. We prayed for a healthy child, and even after she was born handicapped, we prayed for her to get well and believed that our prayers would be answered. But nothing has happened."

And then she demanded, "Why did God let this happen to my husband and me, and to our little baby daughter?"

That young mother's cry echoes the cries of generation after generation. Ever since recorded history man has struggled with the problem of evil, pain, and suffering. Every child is born into a world not of his making, and to parents not of his choosing. And as time passes he encounters pain, injustice, loss, disappointment.

When the storm of suffering hits we try to find the reason; suffering people ask many questions. Why did this have to happen to *me?* Why would God let this happen? Doesn't God hear my prayers? Can't I depend on God to guide me? Is God good if he allows pain and evil?

Is God really all-powerful? Does he perform miracles today? Am I being punished for past sins? Has God turned his back on me? These are just a few examples of the questions my clients have asked me over the years.

Unfortunately, many people carry an additional burden of guilt *because* they ask such questions. They have somehow gotten the impression that if they had the right kind of faith, they would not have doubts or questions about God. Not so. I believe that, in spite of the limits of human insight and intelligence, we must seek to understand the causes of life's difficulties. Such regrettable advice as, "Don't ask why, just believe," or "Have faith and you won't need to understand" only adds to the suffering.

Let's take a look at the Book of Job (the Bible's oldest book), which deals with the problem of human suffering. Job, a great and respected man in his part of the world, *in one day* experienced a number of overwhelming calamities. His vast herds of camels and oxen were stolen and their attending servants killed. At the same time his seven thousand sheep, along with the shepherds Job employed, were killed by a thunderstorm. While this was happening, a cyclone took the lives of all ten of his children. Following these tragedies Job was afflicted with the most bothersome and painful disease known to the ancient world: boils. The culminating assault on his faith came when his own wife advised him to "curse God and die."

Job himself had a great desire to learn *why* all this happened. He did not sit piously on his ash-heap and pretend everything was o.k. He said, "The cause which I knew not I searched out" (29:16).

We must realize that faith is not in conflict with a desire to understand. On the contrary, the mind is one of God's greatest gifts to us and we are taught to use and develop it. Solomon wrote these wise words: "I applied mine heart to know, and to search, and to seek wisdom, and the reason for things . . ." (Eccles. 7:25). And Christ himself urged his followers to "ask . . . seek . . . knock," adding, "For every one that asketh receiveth; and he that seeketh findeth, and to him that knocketh it shall be opened" (Matt. 7:7–8). Those who are suffering and wondering why should be shown compassion and assisted in ways that sustain them.

However, one of the weaknesses of literature dealing with suffering is its preoccupation with logical *reasons,* and its demand for fully satisfying solutions. Many kinds of suffering cannot be merely explained; the human intellectual capacity is too limited. We must realize that suffering is much deeper than the intellect. When these depths of pain are reached the suffering man or woman does not want insulting platitudes—the impotent efforts of logic—but the healing, sustaining influence of love and understanding. And how grateful they are for people who realize their need for help that goes beyond "head answering to head."

Let us return to Jesus' parable of the two foundations for a moment, and consider a third perspective the story reveals. Notice that the storm exposed what kind of foundation each man was building. The two houses in Christ's parable probably *looked* very similar—until the storm hit. In favorable "weather" each person's foundation—his assumptions and beliefs—is untested, and so he may have the appearance of strength and stability. But the storm will always reveal the truth about one's life foundation.

How do we each get our foundation for living? We know that heredity makes an important contribution. Our sex, race, intellectual limits, skeletal structure, eye color, and other biologically-determined features come to us through genetic endowment over which we have no control. More important than heredity, however, is the contribution of environment. For we encounter and are encountered by the external world in ways that greatly influence our first five to seven years.

But even more important than heredity or environment is the way a person directs his own life; the choices he makes. We are created with the freedom to choose. This gift of freedom is both precious and terrible; how we exercise it determines the quality of our foundation. Day by day we are behaving our way toward our self-made destiny.

In their effort to explain evil, pain, and misfortune, people sometimes attempt to distinguish between God's perfect will and God's permissive will, between what God intends and what God allows. This, however, leads to problems. God did create us to be free, and this freedom makes possible both good and evil. But it is vitally important to understand that God's will is identified with the freedom—*not* with the evil resulting from the misuse of that freedom. To associate evil with even the permissive will of God is to fail to clearly distinguish things which differ (Rom. 2:18; Phil. 1:10). God wills our freedom and the obedient exercise of that freedom; he does *not* will evil (Rom. 12:2; 2 Peter 3:9).

Causes of Suffering

What happens when we misuse our freedom to live in harmony with God's plan for our lives? The terrible consequences of choosing to ignore God can be found in the first chapter of Romans. Perhaps no other place in all of literature paints a more frightening picture of what we can do to ourselves. By our wrong choices, we experience moral and ethical breakdown, and trade the potential of knowledge and vision for foolishness and darkness. When there is no place for God in our motives and manner of life, personal and (eventually) social deterioration is the bitter result. Is this a fate *imposed* on man? Is this "the will of God"? Absolutely not. This is solely a result of our rejection of the good will of God.

We must soberly consider that rejecting the will of God, that is, *sinning,* always causes suffering. No teaching in the Bible is clearer than this: "Be not deceived; God is not mocked: for whatsoever a man soweth, that shall he also reap. For he that soweth to his flesh shall of the flesh reap corruption" (Gal. 6:7–8). And this: "Now the works of the flesh are manifest, which are these: adultery, fornication, uncleanness, lasciviousness, idolatry, witchcraft, hatred, variance, emulations, wrath, strife, seditions, heresies, envyings, murders, drunkenness, revelings, and such like: of the which I tell you before, as I have also told you in time past, that they which do such things shall not inherit the kingdom of God" (Gal. 5:19–21).

Sin always causes suffering; however, suffering is not always caused by sin. One of the clearest examples of this truth comes from the biblical account of the healing of the man born blind (John 9:1–7). When the disciples saw the blind man, they asked Jesus, "Rabbi, who sinned, this man or his parents, that he was born blind?" Like so many people before and after them, the disciples associated all suffering with sin. They reasoned that if neither the parents nor the son had sinned, there would be no cause for the blindness.

Jesus' answer must have startled them: "It is not that this man or his parents sinned. But that the works of God might be made manifest in him I must work the works of him who sent me, while it is day" (vv. 3–4).* Instead of

---

*The reader of this verse in the King James Version will notice the difference in punctuation in this passage. Because the New Testament was written in Greek, which was not punctuated, the change in punctuation is not only grammatically permissible but more in harmony with the nature and purpose of God as revealed by Christ and scriptural teaching.

trying to explain the mystery of suffering, Jesus did two
things that were more important. First, he asserted that
God had sent him into the world to make man whole.
God's will is our highest good, and whatever frustrates
the divine purpose for each of us should be understood
as part of the reason Christ was sent to the earth. Second, by healing the blind man, Christ manifested the
love and the power of God to achieve his purpose.

Another reason that people suffer is because we lack
knowledge. What we don't know does hurt us. The field
of medical science has made great strides, but it continues to be baffled by cancer.

Medical research has long assumed that every serious
disease is caused by a germ or virus (a pathological organism). Once the invading organism can be isolated, an
antibiotic can be used to combat the disease. But this
approach does not take into consideration the way the
human body defends itself when confronted with various
kinds of mental and emotional breakdowns.

The "non-germ theory" of cancer is being increasingly
supported by new findings which relate some forms of
cancer to emotional disturbances. For example, we now
know that persistent anxiety and repressed rage often
cause cancer of the stomach or colon. And it is now well
documented that emotional conditions can produce
chemical changes in the body.

However, how can we explain the great variety of ways
people react to stress, tension, and frustration? And how
can people develop more adequate defense patterns?

First we must realize that we frequently bring suffering
upon ourselves—by impulsive decisions, carelessness,
undisciplined living. Jake, a forty-year-old male client, is
typical of irresponsible behavior which leads to suffering.
He willingly spends a fortune seeking the best doctors
hoping to find a cure for an ulcerous stomach. He under-
goes numerous examinations and receives frequent x-ray
treatments. He is even willing to have his stomach re-

moved—anything to be rid of the painful ulcer that obsesses him. Yet, he refuses to follow the doctors' advice to rest and smoke no more cigarettes. How many of us are represented by the man in the following:

> To get his wealth
> He spent his health
> And then with might and main
> He turned around and spent his wealth
>   To get his health again!
>
> —Anonymous

People also suffer because they live in a world with other people. We are all affected by the behavior of others. As the apostle reminds us, "No man liveth unto himself and no man dieth to himself" (Rom. 14:7). In such a world of imperfect people there is no escaping the painful sharing of the consequences of sin, ignorance, and folly.

However, we should not fail to appreciate the *profitable* sharing of the effects of the contribution of others. As an Englishman once noted,

> When I rise and go to my bath a cake of soap is handed me by a Frenchman, a sponge is handed me by a Pacific Islander, a towel by a Turk, my undergarments by one Englishman, my outergarments by another. I come down to breakfast. My tea is poured out by an Indian or a Chinese. My porridge is served by a Scottish farmer, or my corn flakes by Mr. Kellogg and his friends. My toast I accept at the hands of an English farmer who has joined hands with a baker. My marmalade is passed to me by a Spaniard, my banana by a West Indian. I am indebted to half the world before I have finished breakfast.

Yes, belonging to the human family has its blessings as well as its burdens.

Considering some of the major reasons we suffer can

be extremely valuable. But what help is there for the person who, like the foolish man in Jesus' story, has a foundation collapsed?

One of the reasons why the gospel is called good news is that a new and better foundation can be built if the old one has crumbled. For the believer, every crisis is an opportunity for growth.

Gaining insight into the cause of suffering is vitally important; without such insight we continue to repeat the same mistakes. Usually, however, when we know *why* we suffer we are also filled with regret, remorse, and even despair. When our lives contain willful sin, impulsive acts, harsh words, or personal failure, we can become so discouraged that we shrink back from life.

In such times we need to remember the lesson drawn from the experience of Dr. Leslie Weatherhead. As a young British officer in World War I he was assigned to India. While he was there he was able to observe the remarkable skills of the rug-weavers. Passing among the workers, he turned to his guide and asked, "What if the weaver makes a mistake?" The guide replied, "If he is a great enough artist, he will weave the mistake into a pattern." As followers of Christ, we have the assurance that the divine artist is great enough to take even our blunders and weave them into the pattern of a life that will glorify him. For "we know that all things work together for good to them that love God, to them who are the called according to his purpose" (Rom. 8:28).

We Can Face Suffering

Suffering cannot be completely explained, but it must still be faced. And here we come to the critical point. More important than what happens to us is *how we respond* to what happens. We do have the freedom to respond to suffering in a positive way, to make it serve a purpose and give it value. Suffering can impose limits, but it cannot take away our freedom to decide what our attitudes will be.

For our most reliable guidance, we seek our perfect example, Jesus Christ. This time we find him in the Garden of Gethsemane,* and observe what will forever be beyond our ability to grasp. Christ knew he would go to Calvary. He would be beaten, humiliated, and finally crucified. He would bear upon himself the sins of man. His Father would momentarily turn away, leaving the hanging sacrifice to feel forsaken. Physically, mentally, or spiritually, no one has ever suffered like this, before or after Christ. There were dimensions of pain in that cup that we will never understand. Up to a point, each of us can realize the deep significance of this act of love, but then we are filled with a kind of mysterious silence—the deep language of reverence. Christ's suffering was so profound that he said, "My soul is exceeding sorrowful, even unto death" (Matt. 26:38). And Luke, the beloved physician, wrote: "And being in agony he prayed more earnestly: and his sweat was as it were great drops of blood falling down to the ground" (22:44).

Jesus wanted fellowship in his hour of trial, but those who went to the Garden with him—Peter, James, and John—could not stay awake. Jesus was left alone. In the same way, there are times when others can go only so far with us. Some of life's trials have to be borne in the lonely solitude of a person's own soul.

Christ's first response to the idea of the cross was, "If it be possible let this cup pass from me." Our initial reaction when faced with suffering is also to avoid it. We'd rather be comfortable, pain-free, and content. That is *our* will. But consider Christ's next sentence: "Nevertheless, not my will but thine be done." Jesus accepted the will of his Father. In Mark's version, Jesus said, "Abba, Father,

---

*We read about this episode in the life of Jesus in Matt. 26:36–46; Mark 14:32–42; Luke 22:40–46.

all things are possible to thee; remove this cup from me; yet not what I will but what thou wilt" (14:36). After the desire to have the cup removed comes the great acceptance. This acceptance is rooted in the knowledge that God is working his redemptive purpose through the experience and that ultimately his will will be achieved. In this connection we recall the well-known prayer:

> God grant me the serenity to
> Accept the things I cannot change,
> The courage to change the things I can,
> And the wisdom to know the difference.

We learn this great truth from our consideration of Jesus' suffering: that although no one would *choose* life's storms, such suffering can be *used* to serve God's higher purposes. The psalmist said, "That man is blessed who, going through the vale of misery, uses it for a well" (84:6). Used rightly, life's adversities can strengthen us. In Romans we read, "We can rejoice, too, when we run into problems and trials for we know that they are good for us—they help us learn to be patient. And patience develops strength of character in us and helps us trust God more each time we use it until finally our hope and faith are strong and steady" (5:3–4, LB).

This truth bears repeating: It is not life's storms but the right response to them that develops us. As James reminds us: "For when the way is rough, your patience *has a chance* [italics mine] to grow. So let it grow, and don't try to squirm out of your problems. For when your patience is finally in full bloom, then you will be ready for anything, strong in character, full and complete" (1:3–4, LB).

Christian disciples learn that "all chastening seemeth for the present to be not joyous but grievous; yet afterward it yieldeth peaceable fruit" (Heb. 12:11). The "fruits" of pain and suffering rightly borne are as precious as they are costly. As the French proverb states:

"To suffer passes. To have suffered, never passes." New dimensions to understanding, compassion, sensitivity, and courage are added by the proper responses to life's storms and stresses. The person thus educated enters a realm of reality he could never discover any other way. The price for living the untroubled life is a noticeable shallowness and immaturity.

It is significant that the prophet Isaiah tells us of "the valley of vision" (22:5); it is the *valley* that is the place for the glimpse of wonder, greater perspective, and expanded living. Isaiah claims that the windswept summit or scenic hilltop is not where we find the vision. The psalmist agrees when he says, "Thou hast enlarged me when I was in distress" (4:1).

The last stanza of "A Psalm of Life" by Henry Wadsworth Longfellow contains these memorable lines:

> Let us then be up and doing,
> With a heart for any fate;
> Still achieving, still pursuing,
> Learn to labor and to wait.

Longfellow well knew the bitter valley that produced his vision. The young poet had suffered the death of his wife, which left him in a state of loneliness and depression. Longfellow, a college professor at the time, lost all inspiration to write. But as time passed, he experienced a vision in his valley.

So we learn to prefer the valley with its vision instead of the mountain peak without it. This preference does not come cheaply. Our faith will be tested; at times we will agonize with doubts, loneliness, and a deep sense of futility. During these times we must keep our hearts unhardened and turned toward him who is not "an high priest which cannot be touched with the feeling of our infirmities" (Heb. 4:15). Then we will gain the insight of the writer who penned these tender and penetrating lines:

Valley of Sorrow

I came to the valley of sorrow
  And dreary it looked to my view,
But Jesus was walking beside me,
  And sweetly we journeyed through.

And now I look to that valley
  As the fairest that ever I trod,
For I learned the love of my Father,
  I leaned on the arm of my God.

And if some day the Father should ask me
  Which was the best path I trod,
How quickly my heart shall make answer
  "The valley of sorrow, O God!"

—Anonymous

We have scriptural basis for the belief that the sufferings of this life are not permanent. "These troubles and sufferings of ours . . . won't last very long. Yet this short time of distress will result in God's richest blessing upon us forever and ever! So we do not look at what we can see right now, the troubles all around us, but we look forward to the joys in heaven which we have not yet seen. The troubles will soon be over, but the joys to come will last forever" (2 Cor. 4:17–18, LB).

The Christian's hope is based on the knowledge that no valley is endless; no burden will remain unlifted. When time stretches into eternity the deepest yearnings of the human heart will have fulfillment. "Eye hath not seen, nor ear heard, neither have entered into the heart of man the things which God hath prepared for them that love him" (1 Cor. 2:9). And Job, that great Old Testament sufferer, was told, "Thou shalt forget thy misery, and remember it as waters that pass away" (Job 11:16).

In the first part of this chapter we discussed the parable of the two foundations which dealt with life's storms. This brings us to the story of a little girl talking with her father about the storm they had experienced the night before. "Daddy," she asked, "what was God doing last night during the storm?" Then getting a flash of insight, she answered her own question: "I know. God was busy making the morning."

Christians look forward with John to the time of the new heaven and the new earth, when "God shall wipe away all tears from their eyes: and there shall be no more death, neither sorrow, nor crying, neither shall there be any more pain" (Rev. 21:4).

Writing this chapter has stirred painful memories that are very personal. Due to a relatively rare disease, I was born with seeded warts on my vocal cords. My parents were told by the doctors who first examined me that I would never be able to talk out loud. And for the first five years of my life, they were right. I learned to talk by whispering.

As the warts on my vocal chords grew, surgery became necessary. But each time the warts were surgically removed, they grew back thicker than before. Finally, to enable me to breathe, the doctors put a tube in my throat and I breathed through that tube for almost five years. Sleep at night during that time was frequently interrupted because the tube stopped up. I owe my life to my mother, who carefully unstopped the tube nightly for almost five years.

Because I was not allowed to play with other children, my parents were trying to find a teacher to start me in my formal educational program at home. Then a miracle happened. My mother was converted to Christ and told her pastor about me. He prayed for me at the altar and afterward I was taken back to the surgeon who had operated on me numerous times. He looked into my throat and then with amazement asked, "What has happened to this boy? His throat is as clear as a whistle!" He took the tube out of my throat, bandaged my throat, and I've been talking out loud ever since!

Due to the heat from the x-rays, however, one of my

vocal cords never matured. So I have used my one good vocal cord in ministering to people of all ages, in all kinds of churches, camps, and seminars. Over the years, I must confess that this limitation has often been frustrating. To this day, if I speak for forty-five minutes or more, I will be so hoarse that I can hardly make a sound for two or three hours.

Many times I turn to one of my greatest sources of inspiration, the apostle Paul. Writing of his own "thorn in the flesh," he said that he "begged" the Lord to remove the affliction but received this reply: "My grace is enough for you: for where there is weakness, my power is shown the more completely" (2 Cor. 12:9, *Phillips*).

At the age of seventeen, I dived off a pier in Port O'Connor, Texas, and broke my neck. When I realized that my condition was critical, I committed my life to the will of God and after surgery, two and one-half months in the hospital, and six months of wearing a brace, I returned to a normal, active life. Shortly afterward, I met a young man my age who had suffered a broken neck in exactly the same way as I had. Only he lay paralyzed from his neck down. I left his hospital room asking, "Why was he paralyzed and why was I spared?" The answers to such questions are beyond our understanding.

Some twenty-five years later, tumors appeared on my thyroid glands and the diagnosis indicated a good chance that they were malignant. After the first operation my throat collapsed and when I revived, I had another tube in my throat! I was devastated. It seemed I was going to be forced to relive some of the past that I don't willingly recall. After two more operations and three months of hospitalization,* the tube finally came out. This time, I pray, for good.

So when I write about suffering, confusion, frustration,

---

*I gratefully acknowledge the unforgettable way my wife, Mamie, lovingly and faithfully ministered to me during this time.

and related problems, it is not being done from a theological ivory tower. My personal experiences have not given me all the answers. They *have* produced lots of questions. The books on my study shelves contain deep thinking on the mystery of suffering. And my search for answers continues. But of this I'm certain; God is a good God, whose will is our highest good. And life *always* works best when it is lived in harmony with the divine will. So, if I can't understand completely, I can trust, obey, and continue to live for him who promised he would never leave us or forsake us. This concept is powerfully expressed in the following lines:

Footprints in the Sand

One night a man had a dream. He dreamed he was walking along the beach with the Lord. Across the sky flashed scenes from his life. For each scene, he noticed two sets of footprints in the sand; one belonged to him and the other to the Lord.

When the last scene of his life flashed before him, he looked back at the footprints in the sand. He noticed that many times along the path of his life, there was only one set of footprints. He also noticed that it happened at the very lowest and saddest times in his life.

This really bothered him and he questioned the Lord about it. "Lord, you said that once I decided to follow you, you'd walk with me all the way. But I have noticed that during the most troublesome times in my life, there is only one set of footprints. I don't understand why when I needed you most, you would leave me."

The Lord replied, "My precious child, I love you and I would never leave you. During your times of trial and suffering, when you see only one set of footprints, it was then that I gently took you in my arms and carried you."

8

Preventing a Nervous Breakdown

A few years ago instead of writing about nervous breakdowns I was having one! The first serious sign appeared when I walked into my study just before leaving my home in Houston, Texas, to go to Michigan to teach a summer camp. For no apparent reason I suddenly burst into tears and began to tremble all over.

Nothing like this had ever happened to me. In my academic preparation I had studied emotional disturbance and had counseled people who were suffering from it in various ways. But now it was happening to *me.* For an entire summer, while teaching and traveling in several states across the nation, I entered what seemed to be a dark cave that had no light or exit.

This chapter on what is commonly called the nervous breakdown is the result of what I learned during those dark months, and from years of counseling experience with people suffering similar problems.

Obviously, space will not permit a comprehensive, indepth treatment of the subject. But I do hope to succeed in helping the reader to understand what is commonly called the nervous breakdown—what it is, how it happens, what it means, how to overcome it, and how to prevent it.

To help in understanding what a nervous breakdown is, let's take the case of a woman we'll call Janet. When she walked into my consulting room, I readily observed a number of signs that indicated she was experiencing severe emotional distress.

"I feel so embarrassed coming here like this," she began.

"Embarrassed?"

"Yes, you see, I'm a *Christian* and that means that I shouldn't be having these kinds of problems, doesn't it?"

"What kinds of problems?" I asked, preferring to wait until later to explain why Christians can and do have these kinds of problems.*

"I think I'm about to have—or maybe I'm having—a nervous breakdown," she continued in a very deliberate, halting manner. And then came the familiar description: crying for no apparent reason, loss of ability to concentrate, "raw" nerves, sleeplessness, loss of appetite, depression, wanting to avoid people and daily responsibilities, lack of the sense of God's nearness, feeling that prayer is useless, loss of meaning in life (usually accompanied by suicidal thoughts). These are among the most common ways of experiencing the nervous breakdown.

It is interesting to study the language used by people experiencing emotional stress. "I'm going to pieces," "falling apart," "flying off the handle," "coming apart at the seams," "losing my mind," "my nerves are collapsing." Sometimes they refer to themselves as "crackpot," "scatter-brained," "nervous wreck," or claim they are "going crazy." In this connection it is enlightening to consider the origin of the word *crazy*—it comes from the Old English *crasen,* meaning "to break" or "to shatter."

These self-descriptions have a common meaning. The person is experiencing a loss of unity of personality, of inner harmony.

In attempting to define the nervous breakdown, I have found that it is helpful to start by explaining what it is *not.* First, it is not damage to the nerves. Although the

*See chapter 7.

nervous system is disturbed, the nerves themselves do not show any signs of "breakage." Careful, thorough medical examinations have repeatedly confirmed this point so that it is now an established scientific fact.

Second, the nervous breakdown is not a problem that a person is a "victim of." That is, the nervous breakdown is not to be feared in the same way as cancer, for example. As I will point out later, to think of personality disturbance in the same way as we think of physical illness has no basis in either medical science or behavioral science.

Third, the nervous breakdown is not a problem that "God wills" for anyone. Despite the sad fact that some well-meaning Christians believe this, we have no scriptural authority for it.

Now let's look at what a nervous breakdown *is*. A major problem in defining the nervous breakdown is the lack of general agreement among doctors and psychologists. As Dr. William Menninger, the internationally-esteemed psychiatrist, has written: "Nervous breakdown is a term used to include everything from headaches to fallen arches. . . ." He adds that in almost every instance the nervous breakdown is more accurately diagnosed as a mental breakdown accompanied by physical symptoms—insomnia, upset stomach, tremulousness, fatigability, and others, "all of which are partial expressions of the personality."

This chapter presents the point of view that the nervous breakdown is the breaking "up" of a pattern of living—a way of thinking, believing, and behaving—that no longer "works." That is, the life pattern is no longer adequate, and the individual cannot stand the requirements of living in the same way that he used to live. When a breakdown is understood in this way, people who may be experiencing an emotional stress gain hope. *For if a nervous breakdown is a condition that we behave ourselves into, then we can understand it as a condition we can behave ourselves out of.* When life tests a person's pattern of living and a breakdown occurs, it is often understood as a closed door, a dead end, and that kind of thinking adds a sense of helplessness and despair. However, when a person is able to understand it as *an opportunity to grow,* this produces a vastly different response that brings hope and relief.

How Does "Breakdown" Happen?

Once we accept the idea that our problem is one that we have behaved ourselves into, it becomes easier to understand how the "breakdown" happened. Our thinking is clarified by contrasting the fragmented personality with the personality which possesses wholeness and harmony. Simply stated, the person living joyfully, meaningfully, and productively possesses a sense of *unity* in himself. Another word that characterizes him is *integrity,* which is unity of belief and behavior. When this unity of personality corresponds to the principles of life as God wills it to be lived (his will is revealed in the Bible) then a sense of wholeness results. We might use the word *lifestyle* to describe the person's ways of believing, valuing, behaving, and interpreting. Thus, if our lifestyle is in harmony with the truth about how life ought to be lived, then our pattern of living is "working."

However, if our lifestyle is *not* corresponding to the will of God as we are individually and collectively required to live it, then our pattern of living no longer works. It is this breakdown in the pattern of living that reveals the need to reexamine our lifestyles.

A pattern of living that no longer works breaks up when life requires responses that we are unable—or unwilling—to give. This lack of ability to respond to life's requirements is basically caused by stress resulting from conflict in the personality. In most cases this conflict is a problem that the person does not want to recognize. So the person devises a strategy for keeping the conflict from recognition. This strategy is called self-defense, which is basically an effort to maintain *hiddenness.*

In this connection it is extremely helpful to consider the insight of Solomon who wrote, "Every way of a man is right in his own eyes . . ." (Prov. 21:2). As we grow up we learn to develop remarkable methods of protecting our own sense of "right," even if it means deceiving ourselves! But if there is a serious enough disturbance present in the self, self-deception will become more difficult with the passing of time. Thus, aging has a weakening effect on these methods of self-defense. As we get older there is a corresponding loss of ability to supply the kind of energy necessary to continue the deception. And as the ability to continue the deception breaks down, there is a building up of stress related to fear of exposure. The breaking down of the former combined with a building up of the latter eventually results in a collapse. The self feels "splintered," exhausted. In this condition the person can be seriously handicapped; he may find it difficult to carry out the responsibilities of daily life.

Sometimes this breakdown appears to have happened "all of a sudden." Usually the suffering person can refer to a particular stressful problem or perhaps a series of stressful problems occurring over a short period of time. Did these problems *cause* the breakdown? Or did they *reveal* the lack of an adequate pattern of living? "The men in the armed forces don't break down," said a psychiatrist. "They fall to pieces. They were never put together, they were held up by environment, by home, by school and when they were taken away they fell to pieces." In other words, pressure *reveals* rather than *causes* our deficiencies.

What I have explained so far is the failure of self-deception, and its disturbing influence on personality. Truth will fight for recognition and when this *need to be known* conflicts with the *need to cover up,* the stress can accumulate beyond the person's tolerance limit. It is important to understand that emotional distress is not an evil in itself, but rather an effort on the part of the personality to rid itself of an undesirable inner condition. Thus personality breakdown, rather than being a problem, is the result of an attempted but unsuccessful cure.

A remarkable example of this problem is recounted by Dr. Leslie Weatherhead, former pastor of the City Temple in London and internationally known for his ability to help people suffering from nervous disorders with nonphysical causes. In the winter of 1937, Dr. Weatherhead was receiving an average of a hundred letters a day, and he tried to respond to each letter himself. His schedule became so full that he said, "I literally had to look six months ahead in my diary to find half an hour for a soul in trouble." The strain of this life pattern took its toll. With bitter irony he recalled, "After giving ten addresses on nervous breakdown I broke down." For six months he was unable to pastor and entered "a darker hell than I believed existed." Writing of this experience some years later, he said, "I dreaded what is called a nervous breakdown. I dreaded it not only because I knew a lot about it, but because my pride was affected." He continued by confessing his failure to recognize that he allowed himself to be overworked and that "part of [his] overwork was egotism." During his period of recovery, Dr. Weatherhead was under the care of Lord Horder, a friend as well as a physician. Dr. Horder explained to his humiliated friend that knowing a lot of psychology no more saves a person from a breakdown than knowing a lot about medicine saves us from infection. Now a sadder but wiser man, Dr. Weatherhead shared this insight: "I had unwittingly opposed the rules of health and had to pay the price."

The Scriptures declare that God will not allow us to face problems that are greater than we can bear. Therefore when personality disturbance reaches the point of "breakdown," we conclude that something in our pattern of living has gone awry. When life makes requirements that we are no longer able to meet, what reasons are we to give?

Over the years the study of human behavior has been separated from the authority of the Bible. One of the most tragic and harmful effects of this separation is a loss of ability to define the root of man's problems.

Some years ago a large-scale survey entitled *Americans View Their Mental Health* revealed that few people were willing to accept at least a share of the responsibility for their mental and emotional troubles. Modern man much prefers to think that personality disturbance is like an illness caused by a virus.

When the sufferer's problems are understood in terms of physical illness, sickness, or disease, certain implications follow. First, the person views himself as a "victim" of what has happened to him. He is not held responsible for his condition. Second, in order to recover, the person expects—and is expected—to have things done *to* him; drugs may be administered, shock treatment given,* or surgery performed. Third, the "patient" receives special considerations. He may be excused from work, classes, etc. It is not too difficult to understand why many find it easier to "put their back on a couch or bed than their shoulder to the wheel"!

Such persons who view themselves as "victims" suffering from a "sickness" commonly go to the medical doctor, expecting to be treated as patients who have had "something happen to them." The notion that "mental illness" is something like an "enemy invasion of germs" may be less self-condemning but cannot stand the test of biblical knowledge or insight from modern behavioral and medical science.

---

*The reader should be aware of the lack of scientific evidence to support shock treatment. In addition, those who receive shock treatments are deprived of experiencing self-mastery resulting from learning they *can* behave themselves out of their condition.

Now disorders of thought and feelings are being thought of as "problems in living," "inappropriate conduct," "irresponsible behavior," and "sinfulness." Mental illness, according to Dr. Thomas Szasz, a prominent psychiatrist, is a myth and serves only to disguise and then make more "palatable the bitter pill of moral conflicts in human relations."

The point that must not be missed is this: Scripture teaches that each person is responsible for his or her behavior. What we experience as a result of our behavior is an effect with a cause and we are responsible for the way we use our freedom in connection with the cause. "What ever a man soweth that shall he also reap." That each person bears responsibility for his behavior is central to the biblical understanding of man.

But modern thinking has attempted to change this. No longer does our society think in terms of right and wrong; now it is more popular to use the medical term *sickness*. Carefully consider these quotes:

> The most important thing for your patient's chances of recovery and for your own peace of mind is to realize that mental illnesses are illnesses like any others (Stern, Edith M., *Mental Illness*, Harper and Row, 1957).

> If everyone would just realize that mental illness is no different from any other prolonged disease and that a heart attack victim differs only from a mental victim in the localization of the affliction, the psychiatrist-therapist's job would be greatly simplified (*Mind Over Matter*, 1962).

> People with either mental or emotional illness need help from medical specialists just the same as people with pneumonia, or ptomaine (*Some Things You Should Know about Mental and Emotional Illness*).

Strong opposition to this "disease view" is being expressed by prominent behavioral scientists. Dr. O. Hobart Mowrer, a former president of the American Psychological Association, agrees with Anton T. Boisen, who said, "In mental disorders we are dealing with a problem which is essentially spiritual."*

According to the Bible, which in my opinion is our most reliable authority, a *sinful* pattern of living is the most serious cause of breakdown. Experiencing sin's consequences without being able to relate them to their proper cause creates confusion and adds greatly to the problem.

From the scriptures come these insights:

> The wicked man travaileth with pain all his days . . . (Job 15:20).

> Fools because of their transgression, and because of their iniquities are afflicted (Ps. 107:17).

> . . . the way of transgressors is hard (Prov. 13:15).

> Tribulation and anguish, upon every soul of man that doeth evil . . . (Rom. 2:9).

> Destruction and misery are in their ways (Rom. 3:16).

In the words of the late Dr. J. Wallace Hamilton, "This is not a good world to be bad in." The reason is basically simple—we live in a morally ordered universe with cause and effect relationships that never change. And nothing is so injurious to human personality as conscious, deliberate wrong choosing and acting. Every time this is done the moral decay spreads, increasing the likelihood of inner collapse.

But we must go beyond broad generalities. Christ boldly identified the kinds of "evil things" that "come from within, and defile the man." He said that "out of the heart of men proceed evil thoughts, adulteries, fornications, murders, thefts, covetousness, wickedness,

---

*Such statements should not be taken as minimizing the role of the medical doctor. The highly trained and dedicated members of the medical profession are a vitally important part of the total healing ministry. It is important to note that medical doctors, therapists, and ministers are learning to work more closely together as biblical understanding of the whole person—spirit, mind, and body—spreads throughout the health professions.

deceit, lasciviousness, an evil eye, blasphemy, pride, foolishness" (Mark 7:21–22). These are the symptoms of moral decay; it is this kind of behavior that causes anguish and emotional stress.

Can we behave ourselves into a breakdown and not know why? Yes, by self-deception, which rids the conscious mind of painful ideas and emotions. This is how we escape facing them and dealing with them scripturally. This strategy for removing troublesome thoughts and feelings is called repression.

We must not confuse repression with suppression. The latter term defines self-control and emphasizes responsible behavior. It is a healthy, desirable way of *consciously* facing problems and managing them effectively. However, repression is a self-deceiving attempt to live *as if the problem did not exist*.

The greatest barrier to acknowledging and turning from the kind of behavior that has led to personality disturbance is best described by an old-fashioned word—*hypocrisy*.

To get a clearer idea of the meaning of hypocrisy, you need only to consider the following synonyms: insincerity, deceit, treachery, lying, fraud, affectation, duplicity, and undependability. What makes hypocrisy so dangerous is that it is a self-defeating strategy for dealing with sin. Christ himself could not help persons who refused to admit that there was sin in their lives.

No wonder Christ spoke as he did to the scribes and Pharisees: "Woe unto you, scribes and Pharisees, hypocrites! For ye are like unto whited sepulchres, which indeed appear beautiful outward, but are within full of dead men's bones, and of all uncleanness. Even so ye also outwardly appear righteous unto men, but within ye are full of hypocrisy and iniquity" (Matt. 23:27–28).

Some of the most biting sarcasm in Bible literature is the statement Christ made to those not willing to be honest with him and themselves: "They that be whole need not a physician, but they that are sick" (Matt. 9:12). A modern "Pharisee" is the type of person who believes that he needs no help. He considers himself morally "above" his fellow men. And because of this self-deception, he shows himself to have the greatest need of all.

But this pattern of pretending, veiling, concealing cannot be maintained indefinitely. As Scripture tells us, ". . . there is nothing covered, that shall not be revealed, and hid, that shall not be known" (Matt. 10:26). In spite of our hypocritical efforts, the truth will come out. It may come out through headaches, stomach disorders, deep depression—or nervous disorders that lead to breakdown.

Although personality disturbance is usually related to wrong choosing and behaving, it can be caused by a lack of knowledge. An example of this is C. W. Beers, who feared that epilepsy was contagious and that he had caught it from an older brother. As he later described the experience in *A Mind That Found Itself,* the fear led him to falsely believe that his attacks were being concealed from him and that he really was a hopeless epileptic. So great became his anxiety that in a state of despair he threw himself from an upper window in an unsuccessful attempt to take his own life. How sobering to think that a single sentence from an informed person could have spared the suffering Beers ten years of misery!

Overcoming the Nervous Breakdown

As I have pointed out, the nervous breakdown is often mistakenly described as an illness, something that has happened "to" a person. The definition I have presented takes a sharp turn from this erroneous view. Rather than thinking of personality disturbance as an illness of which we are "victims," we should learn to understand that it is the result of an inner protest against a pattern of living that has serious flaws. To overcome the resulting breakdown we must learn to give up the wrong or ineffective ways of valuing, believing, perceiving, responding; we must develop the right, more effective pattern. Therefore, instead of seeking to restore a person who has broken down to his *former* self, we must realize that what is needed is not restoration but *reformation*. The former self needs to change—that is the meaning of the breakdown. Overcoming it requires experiencing the necessary change in the self.

How does this change take place? We can behave ourselves out of personality disturbance when we (1) gain an understanding of the true causes of our difficulty (insight), (2) believe in the possibility of a desirable outcome (hope), and (3) experience help from adequate resources over a long enough period of time (enduring power).

The first step in overcoming the nervous breakdown, insight, has been explored in the first part of this chapter, which discussed the definition and explanation of this disorder. Recognizing the true cause of our problems can be very difficult, for as Jeremiah tells us, "Deep is a man's mind, deeper than all else, on evil bent; who can fathom it?" (17:9). However, we *can* gain productive insight by courageously praying with David: "Search me, O God, and know my heart: try me, and know my thoughts: And see if there be any wicked way in me, and lead me in the way everlasting" (Ps. 139:23–24).

The second step, believing in the possibility of a desirable outcome (hope), might be illustrated by the examples of how two of the most remarkable men in our nation's history experienced and overcame nervous breakdowns.

The first of these examples is that of Abraham Lincoln, who in his early years suffered from depression so severe that he was afraid he would take his own life. Robert Wilson, one of his friends who served as a fellow member of the Illinois state legislature, recalled this period in Lincoln's life: "When by himself, he told me he was so overcome by mental depression that he never dared carry a knife in his pocket; and as long as I was intimately acquainted with him, he never carried a pocketknife."

During his depression, Lincoln wrote: "I am now the most miserable man living. If what I feel were equally distributed to the whole human family, there would not be one cheerful face in the earth. Whether I shall ever be better I cannot tell. I awfully forebode I shall not. To remain as I am is impossible." But Lincoln did recover; we learn that when Lincoln received the gift of a new Bible from a friend, he wrote, "I intend to read it regularly when I return home. I doubt not that it is really . . . the best cure for the 'blues' could one but take it according to the truth."

Lincoln's estimate of the great contribution the Bible made to his life is made clear by an episode some three years later. Shortly before his assassination, Lincoln invited his long-time friend, Joshua Speed, to his home to spend the night. Speed wrote, "As I entered the room, near night, he was sitting near a window intently reading his Bible. And this remarkable conversation followed:

> Speed: "I am glad to see you so profitably engaged."
> Lincoln: "Yes, I am profitably engaged."
> Speed: "Well, if you have recovered from your skepticism, I am sorry to say I have not."
> Lincoln (looking Speed earnestly in the face and placing his hand on his shoulder): "You are wrong, Speed; take all of this Book upon reason that you can, and the balance on faith, and you will live and die a happier man."

Another prominent man, William James, a noted philosopher who is sometimes called the father of American psychology, experienced a breakdown and he, too, came out of it stronger than ever. While living in Germany, at the age of twenty-five, James suffered for several years in a state of semi-invalidism. During this time he was tortured by obsessions with nameless dreads, disturbed by philosophical doubts, fearful of life and of the horrible possibility of ending up in an institution for the insane. In his *Letters,* he reports his own experience:

> "In general I dreaded to be left alone. I remember wondering how other people could live, how I myself had ever lived, so unconscious of the pit of insecurity beneath the surface of life. My mother in particular, a very cheerful person, seemed to me a perfect paradox in her unconsciousness of danger, which you may well believe I was very careful not to disturb by revelations of my own state of mind."

He added that his feelings of insecurity were "so invasive and powerful that, if I had not clung to scripture-texts like 'The eternal God is my refuge,' etc., 'Come unto me all ye that labor and are heavy-laden,' etc., 'I am the Resurrection and the Life,' etc., I think I should have grown really insane."

When we consider the third way of overcoming the nervous breakdown, power—experiencing help from adequate resources over a long enough period of time—we do well to think about the resources found in Christ's church. The resource most helpful to many disturbed persons is identified by James, who wrote: "Confess your faults one to another . . . that ye may be healed" (5:16).* Following that admonition, we must take seriously a commonly-observed need of the suffering person—the need to confess, to reveal. When an individual's personality disturbance is severe enough to result in serious or complete loss of ability to function, he is often experiencing the futility of hiddenness, dishonesty, hypocrisy. When this concealment underlies the problem, we must allow the person to verbalize his internal condition as far as he is honestly and sincerely able, no matter how great

---

*Great caution must be used in selecting a person to hear a confession. As one teacher advised, "Never take your wounds to anybody but a healer." See chapter 2 for a more fully developed treatment of confession.

the self-reproach becomes. We must learn, as William James used to say, "to exteriorize our rottenness." To discourage an emotionally troubled person's references to misconduct is to fail to recognize that he is trying to find a more effective way of living (he is trying to be *more* moral, *more* responsible, *more* mature). Whether the person is actually describing sin can only be reliably recognized by reference to the Scriptures.

Recently one of my clients shared this remarkable account that led to her complete loss of ability to function as a wife and mother. The trouble began when she became pregnant. At this time she and her husband were struggling financially and were not ready for parenthood. The husband reacted with alarm and the wife felt that she was to blame. Instead of feeling during her first pregnancy "the way a mother-to-be *should* feel," she was growing more resentful with each passing week. "When the baby was born, I actually resented him," she confessed tearfully. "I guess I actually blamed him for the barrier that seemed to separate my husband and me." Being a Christian, she suffered great guilt and self-reproach. Before long she sank into the state of depression that eventually led to her being hospitalized.

Recalling this, with her husband listening attentively, she turned to him and said, "I've never really told you how I felt about this." Neither had she disclosed these painful thoughts and emotions to anyone else. And as time passed the deepening depression served two purposes. First, the depression separated the guilt and self-reproach from her conscious mind, giving her a sense of relief, but making it more and more difficult to associate the depression with its cause. Second, the depression served as a means of self-punishment. By her suffering she was atoning for the agonizing sense of moral rupture. Now, however, the truth was confessed. Her husband forgave her and in a later session she exclaimed, "My relationship with my son has changed remarkably!"

How much suffering could be spared by learning how to talk about our troubles to the appropriate persons! The disturbing power of unasked questions, of the *unuttered* is far greater than is often realized.

In recovering from a breakdown, there is no substitute for learning to live *one day at a time*. The two worst days in the week are yesterday and tomorrow. "*This* is the day which the Lord hath made . . . ," said David (Ps. 118:24). And Jesus himself reminds us, "Sufficient unto the day is the evil thereof" (Matt. 6:34). As an unknown writer poetically puts it:

> Life is hard by the yard;
> But by the inch it's a cinch!

From the life of the famous writer Thomas Carlyle comes a lesson for anyone needing to learn the "inch" approach to life. Carlyle gave his neighbor, the philosopher John Stuart Mill, his complete manuscript on the French Revolution to read. The next morning Mill's maid used the manuscript to start a fire. Imagine Carlyle's reaction! How would he ever reproduce such a project? Later he sat watching a mason building a long brick wall. How did the work progress? One brick at a time. This, thought Carlyle, was the key. Inspired by the insight, he said, "I'll just write one page today—then one page at a time." The result was a finished work that Carlyle felt was better than the first effort.

Dr. William Barclay tells of a little group of people in the Scottish Highlands who were discussing the subject of heroism. They reached the conclusion that everybody sooner or later had to practice some kind of heroic behavior. A young man turned to a serene old woman. Unknown to the young man she had experienced a series of tragedies. "And what kind of heroism do you practice?" he taunted, obviously believing that she was too ordinary to be heroic. But her reply was magnificent: "I?" she said, "I practice the heroism of going on."

By practicing the "heroism of going on" we learn the importance of disciplining the will to *act*. As Goethe once said, "Action—there is courage, magic in it. Anything you can do or think you can, begin it. Once started, the mind grows heated. Begin the job and the work will be completed."

Another source of power is identified by Dr. Alexis Carrel, Nobel Prize-winning physician honored for success in suturing blood vessels. Dr. Carrel said:

Prayer is . . . the most powerful form of energy that one can generate. The influence of prayer on the human mind and body is as demonstrable as that of secreting glands. Its results can be measured in terms of increased physical buoyancy, greater intellectual vigor, moral stamina, and a deeper understanding of the realities underlying human relationships. . . . As a physician, I have seen men, after all other therapy had failed, lifted out of disease and melancholy by the severe effort of prayer. It is the only power in the world that seems to overcome the so-called laws of nature.

And Dr. Hyslop of Bethlehem Mental Hospital, London, stated: "As one whose whole life has been concerned with the suffering of the human mind, I believe that of all the hygienic measures to counteract depression of spirits, and all the miserable results of a distracted mind, I would undoubtedly give first place to the simple habit of prayer."

David was no stranger to personality disturbance. He encountered depression and even violence in King Saul. But his inspired thoughts contain insight, hope, and power for modern sufferers needing help. Earlier in this book I used this inspiring passage:

Happy are they who, nerved by thee,
   set out on pilgrimage!
When they pass through Wearyglen,

fountains flow for their refreshing,
  blessings rain upon them;
They are the stronger as they go,
  till God at last reveals himself in Sion (Ps. 84:5–7,
    Moffatt).

When I recall my "Wearyglen" experience, I remember how encouraging it was to realize that it wasn't permanent, that I would "pass through" it. By learning to live scripturally one day at a time, doing what I could, seeking Christian counsel, praying for guidance and strength, I found those "fountains" that "flow for their refreshing." And further, I discovered the truth of David's statement, "They are the stronger as they go." And any reader of this chapter can discover this truth!

Preventing the Nervous Breakdown

What kind of counsel should be given to readers seeking to develop a successful pattern of living in a world that seems to be increasingly unstable, a world full of rapid change, without a sense of direction?

Modern life was accurately described in Lewis Carroll's *Through the Looking-Glass*. Perhaps you recall the episode involving Alice and the Red Queen in the garden of living flowers. After their introduction to each other, the queen takes Alice by the hand and off they go as fast as their legs can carry them. Poor Alice can't stand the pace and pleads for rest, but the queen only cries, "Faster! Faster!" In spite of their exhausting efforts, however, they seem to be making no progress. When Alice breathlessly points this out to the queen, she gets this intriguing explanation: "Now, here, you see, it takes all the running you can do, to keep in the same place. If you want to get somewhere else, you must run twice as fast as that!"

Carroll's garden of the living flowers sounds remarkably like our own time, doesn't it! And since no one seriously believes that we can gear down our world's pace, we must look for more effective ways of keeping up without breaking down. Our search may well begin by listening to one of the world's greatest physicians, Dr. William Osler. In speaking to the students at Yale in 1913, Dr. Osler stated that "the failure to cultivate the power of peaceful concentration is the greatest single cause of mental breakdown." And students at Harvard used to hear William James say: "Neither the nature nor the amount of our work is accountable for the frequency and severity of our breakdowns, but their cause lies rather in those absurd feelings of hurry and having no time, in that breathlessness and tension . . . that lack of harmony and ease. . . ."

The insight shared by these two men of international prominence was also understood by one who could have been a Phi Beta Kappa in any modern university. In his lifetime, David earned these titles: musician, poet, scholar, military strategist, political leader. A careful study of the matchless psalms of David reveals the key to his genius. Consider these samples: "O God, thou art my God; early will I seek thee . . . (63:1). Let the words of my mouth, and the meditation of my heart, be acceptable in thy sight, O Lord, my strength, and my redeemer (19:14). My heart was hot within me; while I was musing the fire burned . . . (39:3). My meditation of him shall be sweet: I will be glad in the Lord" (104:34). There can be no doubt that David's remarkable life drew great amounts of nourishment from his habit of meditating on his Lord in moments of quietness.

But our search takes us to a greater example than David. Mastering the art of living is primarily a matter of identifying with the Master of life. For to be identified with the One who, more than any other, penetrated life's secrets is to share in his life of power and poise. Followers of Christ can see in him the way to have serenity with service, peace with productivity, insight with involvement. He perfectly exemplified a uniquely balanced life, including in his strenuous schedule a regular period of spiritual renewal. Christ's biographers did not fail to notice the devotional habits of their Master. Matthew gives these samples: ". . . he went up into a mountain apart to pray . . ." (14:23). "And Jesus departed from thence, and . . . went up into a mountain and sat down there . . ." (15:29). Mark shares this: "And he said unto them, Come ye yourselves apart . . . and rest a while . . ." (6:31). And Luke penned this: "And he was withdrawn from them . . . and kneeled down, and prayed" (22:41).

No one has ever broken down when he or she possessed inner calmness. Fear and frenzy are the two worst enemies of serenity and wholeness. Together they create excessive stress which causes the adrenal glands to produce physiological responses associated with nervousness. But fear and frenzy can be mastered by faith and patience, which Jesus said enables us to "possess our souls." Read carefully the following lines which I have personally found helpful and which I have often shared with others whose pilgrimage involves the need for finding serenity of soul:

> Drop thy still dews of quietness,
> Till all our strivings cease,
> Take from our souls the strain and stress,
> And let our ordered lives confess
> The beauty of thy peace.
>
> —John Greenleaf Whittier

Far too many find themselves in the situation of the young man who entered into the following conversation with William Gladstone, one of England's most distinguished prime ministers:

"Young man," said Gladstone, "tell me of your dreams for the future."

"I plan, sir, to go to Oxford."

"I am glad to hear it. What then?"

"Then, sir, I would like to go into law."

"Then?"

"I would like to get married and have a family."

"Fine. What next?"

"I would like to go into parliament."

"A good ambition. And then?"

"Then I suppose I shall retire and read a bit."

"What next?"

"Sir, I have not thought beyond that."

"Young man, you are a fool. Go home and think life through."

We should realize that our lives have eternal significance: *this* life is temporary. We are not prepared to live until we are prepared to die. The best way to live is to face life's experiences according to the highest, most reliable authority, the Bible. There is no power capable of pulling a person together like the knowledge that we are biblically prepared to face life, death, and the life hereafter. Any alternative to this preparation undermines the soul's stability. There is nothing that disturbs personality as much as questions of our own existence—why am I here, where am I going—if they are unanswered or inadequately answered.

The pattern of life that works in our kind of world is rooted in a biblically-defined relationship to Christ and in the principles presented and explained in the Scriptures. How stabilizing it is in our confused, anxiety-ridden world to hear his words: "Let not your heart be troubled . . . believe . . . in me" (John 14:1).

9

Finding Help
Through Counseling

A call for you," announced my receptionist, adding, "someone needs to ask you some questions."

"I think I need help," the caller (a troubled woman) began with some nervous hesitation, "but I'm not sure what kind. What kind of doctor are you?"

"My doctorate is in psychological counseling, and I am certified as a marriage and family therapist," I replied.

"Is that the same thing as a psychiatrist?" she asked. "I guess I'm confused about how one kind of professional therapist differs from another."

I assured her that her confusion was quite common. Like a great number of others seeking professional help (more than twelve million this year), she needed vital information. How do you know when you need help? How do you select a helper? Who are the helpers and how do they differ? How can you receive the maximum benefits from the helper's service? Within this chapter are some of the answers to these questions.

When Do We Seek Help?

How do we know when to seek help for our personal problems? This question can lead to a very complicated discussion, but there are some basic guidelines we can use in finding answers. First, no one develops a pattern of living that enables him to successfully cope with life all the time. We have not gone very far in life's school if we have

159

not made this discovery. Sooner or later life gets too big, demands too much, and our personal limitations are exposed. The difference between what life is requiring and what we are able to give is our problem—or our opportunity to grow (you can see what a great difference our attitude makes!). This chapter is a brief attempt to identify and describe counseling as one kind of solution. Counseling can be understood as a certain path that one can take from the present condition to a more desirable one.

The kinds of problems that cause people to seek help can come in various forms. Sometimes people need more information. As the Old Testament prophet lamented, "My people are destroyed for a lack of knowledge" (Hos. 4:6). It is common for a person to need assurance that what he's experiencing is "normal." Then there are times when life makes an unpredictable turn—a sudden death, an illness, a loss of relationship, job, or opportunity—and a need for crisis counseling is felt. Also, people realize the need for assistance in changing attitudes, values, habits, or patterns of living. Often a knowledgeable physician will refer a person with the physical problem that is caused by some disturbance in the personality to someone skilled in dealing with psychosomatic problems. Marriage and family conflicts cause a great many people to feel a need for help, perhaps to get a different point of view or to be reminded of what is known but not yet understood.

Many people suffer from guilt, many kinds of phobias, and a sense of being separated from God and from other people. Frequently people describe their situation by simply saying, "I am stuck." Other ways of describing this frustration are, "I'm bogged down," "I'm on a dead-end street," or as one of my clients put it, "My life is like being in a quagmire of quicksand: the more I struggle to get out, the deeper I sink."

And there is a long list of more specific problems such as depression, job conflicts, educational problems, problems in dealing with people, loss of self-esteem, repeated failures, nervous conditions that have no physical cause, fear, guilt, and so on. A large number of my clients are seeking to develop more adequate ways of understanding and dealing with suffering.*

Resistances to Seeking Help

Coming to the point where we decide we need help is just the first step, however. The next step is to overcome resistance to actually seeking help. This resistance can sometimes be a greater problem than those for which the troubled person consciously wants help. (Actually these problems are often closely related and may have a common source.) For example, there is the concern for what other people will think. This fear takes the form of wondering, "If I seek counseling I may be regarded as abnormal, weird, or weak." In this case, as in so many others like it, we do well to remember that "the fear of man bringeth a snare . . ." (Prov. 29:25).

One of the strongest resistances is the fear of opening ourselves to another person. I'm continually amazed by what we can do to keep others from knowing certain kinds of things we have done, felt, thought, intended, or experienced. I remember reading about a sociologist who made a careful study of embezzlers. Most of these men were well educated and came from good families. Why would they steal money from their banks and companies? The sociologist's conclusion was based on this discovery: In almost every case they had a problem that they believed they could not share with anyone. Their crime was linked with the belief that they could not talk to anyone about their problem.

Another resistance is the fear of having to accept responsibility for one's own behavior. The stigma attached

*See chapters 2, 7, and 8.

to seeking help when that means "I'm responsible for my own behavior" is very real to a great many people. One of the reasons is that we have strong negative reactions to accepting blame. It is interesting to note that we don't have this resistance when we are suffering physically and seek the help of a medical doctor. As a "patient" our sickness is the result of what has happened "to" us. Thus we do not feel responsible. As a "client," however, when we are having problems in living, something may need changing "in" us. Maybe our values are wrong, or we're immature, or we've developed wrong habits. Perhaps our problems have resulted from trying to follow some advice that turned out to be wrong. Whatever the reason, there is a vast difference in meaning between the terms *patient* and *client.* As patients, we receive treatment; as clients we must reveal ourselves and assume responsibility for our intentions, choices, and behavior.

This kind of resistance is rooted in our ego, our pride. Some people can hardly admit that they need help. They mistakenly believe, "If I seek counseling, I'm inadequate, dumb, irresponsible, bad, a loser." And the male ego is by far the worst offender. Most men cling stubbornly to the belief that a "real man" can solve his own problems and only weak people "have" to go to others for help. Probably no misconception of strength has done more to prevent troubled men from getting help than this one. As I will describe later in this chapter, true counseling involves being able to open ourselves to another in ways that require a great deal of strength. People who are unwilling to do this when it is appropriate and desirable are revealing weakness, not strength.

All too often we fail to seek help when we should because we don't want to lean on others too much. To avoid this we put off seeking help, thinking that we can work our way out by ourselves. But some problems get worse with time, and to delay getting help can make the solutions more difficult to find.

From time to time one encounters resistance when a fee is involved. The idea that a helper whose counseling is his livelihood should charge for his services is generally understood and accepted. Occasionally, however, some people do resist this. Their resistance is usually formed without consideration of the value of certain kinds of counseling. To protect the public from self-proclaimed, unqualified therapists, most states have established very rigid standards for professional helpers. Meeting these standards requires many years of education, which is very expensive. Counseling is usually time-consuming; it requires that careful thought be given not just to the amount of time, but also to the quality of time.

One of the most common resistances is the mistaken belief that Christians should not have problems great enough to require help from another person. How often have I heard, "Just pray and believe and you can solve your problems without needing anyone else!" With this advice comes the implied rebuke: If you *do* have to go to another person, you don't have enough faith, or you are not "where you ought to be," spiritually speaking. When we think clearly about this, we realize that prayer and belief should be responses to the will of God. And God has chosen to use human beings through whom he serves his purposes. Ironically enough, it is often these very people—ministers, teachers, officers, spiritual leaders— who, because of their "image," resist seeking help.

In spite of our increased understanding of the need for and the benefits of counseling, many people still believe that seeking help is something to be ashamed of. I've grown accustomed to hearing troubled believers begin with an apology: "I'm sorry to admit this but I'm a Christian and. . . ." I'm complimented by numbering among my clients clergymen and their wives, and I've come to expect prefatory statements such as, "I'm a minister but here I am in a counselor's office."

In my opinion the most important reason for seeking

help comes from the highest authority for living—the Bible. In the book of wisdom, we find the following:

> Where no counsel is, the people fall: but in the multitude of counsellors there is safety (Prov. 11:14).
>
> The way of a fool is right in his own eyes: but he that hearkeneth unto counsel is wise (Prov. 12:15).
>
> With the well advised is wisdom (Prov. 13:10).

Thus from the book of books comes our encouragement to seek help. But there is one critical point to note. We must be certain that this help is the right kind. Once we believe that the Bible is our highest authority, we take seriously the claim of Christ, who said, "I am the way, the truth, and the life" (John 14:6). The counsel that "works" meets these standards: it moves us in the way of Christ—his way and manner; it is based on biblical principles; it promotes life both here and hereafter.

Any counsel that fails to meet these standards is to be rejected. The main reason is that the questions of why and how to live are involved and the answers to such questions require authority greater than mere opinion. When my clients ask, "What do you think I should do?" I reply, "What I think about it isn't important. Let's find out what the Scriptures set forth and then ask for wisdom to apply the relevant teaching to your situation." The Bible is our divine revelation of truth. The Bible has the answers to life's problems and can always be relied upon to guide us in the way of Christ, in the truth of Christ, and in the life of Christ.

How to Select a Helper

Where do troubled people go when they need help with special personal problems? Some years ago an attempt was made to find an answer to this question. A cross section of the American adult population was studied. The researchers found that one out of every seven Americans has sought professional help for a personal problem. Of this number, 42 percent went to clergymen, 29 percent to physicians, 18 percent to psychiatrists and psychologists, and 10 percent to a special agency or marriage counseling service.

How were these helpers selected? How do troubled people link the help needed with the appropriate helper? If the problem is a toothache, we go to the dentist. If the problem is eyesight, we go to the optometrist. But whom do we consult when a marital crisis arises or when a child is rebelling against school authorities?

The problem is further complicated when we realize that physical problems can be caused by a disturbance within the personality. This kind of problem is called psychosomatic, which comes from the Greek words *psyche,* meaning "mind," and *soma,* meaning "body." The term thus refers to the mind-body relationship. Dr. Roy W. Menninger, president of the internationally-known Menninger Foundation in Topeka, Kansas, estimates that 80 percent of the complaints people take to their doctors—colds, upset stomach, back pains, loss of appetite, insomnia, fatigue—are not physically caused ills as much as they are psychosomatic reactions to problems of living.

With other noted authorities, Dr. Menninger believes that emotional tensions and anxieties are contributing directly to the rising rate of serious illnesses. He states, "As people try to cope with new lifestyles, they often end up smoking, eating poorly, turning to alcohol or drugs, and failing to exercise properly." In spite of the progress of medical science, we are seeing more heart disease, cancer, accidents, strokes, and lung disease—and these are problems that frequently can be traced to the manner in which people are living. In *None of These Diseases,* Dr. S. I. McMillen, a Christian physician, indicates that medical science recognizes that guilt, fear, sorrow, envy, re-

sentment, and hatred are disturbances in the personality
that are responsible for the majority of our sicknesses.

But the difficulties related to physical and emotional
problems are not the only reason that finding the right
helper can be confusing. Another equally confusing reason is clearly illustrated by a letter to Dear Abby. A
reader wrote that one of her married friends had con-
sulted a "marriage counselor" who had advertised in a
newspaper. The counselor told this woman to find a boy-
friend and to join a nudist colony. (He claimed to be a
member of the colony, and showed his client copies of
the colony's magazine.) The woman paid for a year's
counseling in advance, and in five weeks returned to the
office for an appointment. The counselor had moved and
left no forwarding address.

The reader went on to say that she realized all marriage counselors are not dishonest, and asked how a person should select a reputable counselor.

Abby suggested that a person ask his or her family
doctor, clergyman, or the Better Business Bureau. If there
is a university in one's town, she added, the head of the
psychology department can offer a recommendation.
Also, the American Association of Marriage and Family
Therapists, 225 Yale Avenue, Clairmont, CA 91711, can
recommend a counselor in one's area.

The nationally syndicated columnist's advice invites us
to take a closer look at the helpers and their qualifications. Let's consider these helpers in the order described
in the national study referred to earlier.

The minister. Today's minister spends a great deal of his
time counseling people with a wide range of personal
problems. Fortunately, more and more ministers are being trained to counsel. However, there is still a lack of
uniformity in the educational preparation of ministers.
Some have not graduated from high school; others have
earned doctoral degrees. The present trend among programs designed to train ministers is encouraging, with

increased attention being given to the role of the minister as counselor. Because of his availability, training, and personal gifts, the modern clergyman will continue to rank high on the list of helpers. The well-trained minister can advise people about crucial choices (for example, selecting a mate or joining a church); marital problems; parenting (learning Christian nurture or dealing with family conflicts); transitional adjustments (changing jobs or planning retirement); crises (coping with the death of a loved one or trying to break an addiction); or sickness (adjusting to a physical handicap or facing surgery). In addition, he can refer people to competent Christian professionals—a physician, lawyer, therapist, or financial counselor.

The physician. Because of the lack of time, today's medical doctor is not always able to give effective counseling. His diagnosis and treatment are limited—not always by choice—to the physical problems of his patients. A doctor can be, however, a valuable source of referral for people who are seeking help with problems of a nonphysical nature.

The psychiatrist. The helpers most commonly confused are the psychiatrist and the psychologist. Although these two terms are often used interchangeably, they refer to two very different groups of professionals. The psychiatrist is a medical doctor who has taken additional training in the treatment of mental disorders. Unlike the other members of the helping professions, the psychiatrist can prescribe medicine. He or she must be licensed to practice medicine in his state. Because of his or her training, the psychiatrist has expertise in identifying the medical implications of a person's emotional problems.

The psychologist. Psychologists devote most of their time to trying to understand the cause of personality problems or problems in living. Although the psychologist is not allowed to prescribe medicine, his training in understanding human growth and development gives special insight into a wide range of problems that require a non-medical approach. The psychologist is usually a doctor of psychology.

Psychologists are trained to use psychological tests to aid in identifying problems. These tests include those that measure mental ability, aptitude, achievement, personality, interest, and so on.

Some of the special fields in psychology can be identified and briefly described.

Clinical psychology is the study and treatment of behavioral problems that are considered quite severe.

Counseling psychology involves helping persons whose problems are less severe than those treated by the clinical psychologist.

Educational psychology is the specialty that deals with students who have learning difficulties and with finding ways of improving the overall educational process. School psychologists provide counseling and guidance to students.

Developmental psychology is concerned with the changes of behavior that occur as we move through the different states of development of our life.

The psychotherapist. A psychotherapist may be a doctor of philosophy, a doctor of education, or a master of social work, and differs from the psychologist primarily regarding his extensive training in supervised counseling.

The social worker. The psychiatric social worker is trained to practice psychotherapy, usually but not always under a doctor's supervision, has the Master of Social Work degree, and is accredited by the Academy of Certified Social Workers. The psychiatric social worker acts as liaison between the medical team and the patient's family, and makes home visits to evaluate and advise on matters relative to improving conditions conducive to building better interpersonal relationships. These social workers serve in local mental-hygiene clinics, child-guidance clinics, or the outpatient department of psychiatric care provided by tax-supported city or state hospitals. They also work in adoption agencies, orphanages, maternity homes, institutions for delinquents, and other children's-welfare institutions. It is also important to know that the federal government uses social workers to provide aid to disabled adults and vocational rehabilitation to civilians. Additional aid given to dependent families, children, the aged, and the blind is provided through local welfare workers who are trained in social work.

The marriage counselor and the family therapist. Because of the widespread breakdown of marriage and the family in our nation, qualified helpers in this field are desperately needed. The American Association of Marriage and Family Therapists certifies persons who have met rigid educational requirements and have spent at least two years in a supervised internship program. In states that license counselors, the certified counselor has passed the state licensing examination.

The paraprofessional or trained lay person. One of the most promising trends in churches involves the use of selected persons who receive special training in the scriptural approach to counseling. A growing amount of research is showing that nonprofessional people who show sensitivity, understanding, and a willingness to be trained can be developed to become excellent "mental-health counselors" or "people helpers." Because they have the traits associated with effective helping, these persons often are *more* successful than professionals! Sometimes called paraprofessionals, these gifted persons are trained by and work under the supervision of a professional therapist who is a deeply committed Christian. These training programs, offered in churches and Bible colleges, are producing "helpers" with resources capable of handling most of the counseling done in local churches.

These persons may be found by contacting Bible colleges, churches, Christian day schools and widely known television programs such as the 700 Club and P.T.L.

The Importance of the Right Choice

You can tell what kind of advice a person wants by the kind of counselor he or she chooses. *Christian counselors give Christian advice.* Christ declared, "I am the way, the truth, and the life." If he is taken seriously then we conclude that our choices are basically two: We can choose *the* way or we can choose *a* way. This choice must be clearly understood if we are to live with intelligence. Every possible effort must be made to understand that if we take Christ seriously there is no neutral ground. The uncompromising standard for the Christian believer is whether our choice takes us in the way that is biblically defined and Christ-controlled.

But some may ask, "Are the resources, the help that I need, available if I apply this kind of standard?" To make the discovery that *God has provided the resources for every believer* is one of life's greatest experiences. Where are these resources? In the church, the body of Christ, the community of believers that is instructed in the Word, led and energized by the Holy Spirit, and committed to loving and dedicated service to Jesus Christ who reigns as Savior and Lord.

The Christian should begin his search for help by realizing that God has provided resources in the church. "And God hath set some in the church, first apostles, secondarily prophets, thirdly teachers, after that miracles, then gifts of healings, helps, governments, diversities of tongues" (1 Cor. 12:28). These resources have been provided "for the perfecting of the saints, for the work of the ministry, for the edifying of the body of Christ: till we all come in the unity of the faith, and of the knowledge of the Son of God, unto a perfect man, unto the measure of the stature of the fulness of Christ: that we henceforth be no more children, tossed to and fro, and carried about with every wind of doctrine, by the sleight of men, and cunning craftiness, whereby they lie in wait to deceive; but speaking the truth in love, may grow up into him in all things, which is the head, even Christ" (Eph. 4:12–15).

How are these gifted individuals identified? They are recognized first by their training. A burden is not enough. Those persons who have been gifted to help and who desire to help will seek to learn as much as possible about helping. How much training is enough? We can never learn too much; no matter how much training we get, we should continue to develop our abilities and deepen our understanding. Those who follow this pattern give evidence of being "people helpers."

These people are also recognized by their reputation for living a consistent Christian life. The difference between training and character is crucial. Without making the mistake of expecting perfection in others, we must realize that people are helped more by what helpers are than by what they know. Others cannot be helped beyond the level of their helpers.

Why the Counselor's Values Are Important

What a counselor believes is critical. Research has shown that a counselor's values become the standard used to evaluate a client's progress. If the client's behavior changes in the direction approved by the counselor, the client receives the counselor's commendation. This is fine *if* the counselor's standard is the truth; that is, the standard set forth in the Scriptures. When our beliefs regarding moral decisions—what is right and wrong—are being influenced by another person, we cannot be too careful in making sure that we are being influenced in the right direction. And we cannot be reminded too often

that when help involves *how* we live and *why* we live,
that help must be based on reliable authority.

Christian and non-Christian counselors differ in another important way. In addition to differences in values,
the non-Christian's goal often is to help the client to learn
how to help himself, to manage his own life more effectively. This is called autonomy (self-directed, self-man-
aged) and is a noble goal, *as far as it goes*. But to the
Christian counselor, autonomy is not enough. The Christian counselor wants the client to learn how to help himself, to make wiser decisions, to solve his problems and
satisfy his needs more effectively. But the Christian counselor's goal goes beyond this. As Christians, we are
taught by the Scriptures (our highest authority) that we
develop the best kind of autonomy when we make the
will of God our highest aim. This truth was never made
more clear than when Christ declared in the Sermon on
the Mount, "But seek ye first the kingdom of God, and
his righteousness; and all these things shall be added
unto you" (Matt. 6:33). When our lives become God-
directed—this is called theonomy—we learn better self-
direction as a by-product. We might say theonomy is
autonomy according to the will of God. Thus the Christian counselor differs from the non-Christian in that his
goals include those of the non-Christian, but go far beyond them. Life is always best lived when it is submitted
to the highest authority and energized by the personal
relationship developed with the living Christ. Christian
counseling is based on the most reliable authority ever
made available to man. And this is why Christian counseling is so highly valued. Insight that comes from the
Scriptures provides the most reliable way of making decisions and solving problems. And the Holy Spirit reveals
Christ in our hearts and minds so that in addition to
knowing what to do, we receive the power to do it. As
the inspired apostle wrote in what is one of my favorite

verses, "For it is God which worketh in you both to will and to do of his good pleasure" (Phil. 2:13).

So when we seek help that is defined in connection with *the* way, the first and most important question is this: "Is this person a follower of Jesus Christ and is the Bible his ultimate standard for what he believes and how he behaves?" If you are not sure of the answer to this question, do not hesitate to ask.

Next you will need to know about the helper's qualifications and experience. Ask about things such as professional memberships. For example, a psychiatrist would be listed with the American Board of Psychiatrists, a psychologist with the State Board of Health Examiners, a marriage and family therapist with the American Association of Marriage and Family Counselors.*

Also you will want to ask about the cost and the method of payment. Some therapists have a fixed fee, while others charge according to the person's ability to pay (a sliding-scale fee). Because of the difficulty of collecting fees, an increasing number of therapists are requesting payment at each visit. However, most therapists are willing to work out a payment plan with clients who demonstrate financial responsibility.

Be sure to find out if your insurance policy provides coverage for health services provided by qualified professionals. Medicaid programs provide assistance to those who are under twenty-one or over sixty-five, or if you are between twenty-six and sixty-five and handicapped. Full coverage is provided if the therapist is a medical doctor. If help is sought in a clinic or an institute, coverage is provided if the clinic or institute is state-certified and there is a certified psychiatrist on the staff.

Properly qualified helpers welcome new clients' questions about qualifications, values, fees, and techniques.

---

*A list of professional associations is given at the end of this chapter.

So do not worry about frankly discussing these important matters; they should be clearly understood as an important part of the development of the relationship with the helper you finally select.

A common problem that many Christians have is in deciding to go to a therapist or to a minister. The couch or the altar? Such a question is usually based on the false idea that psychology and theology are enemies, or at best hopelessly divided into two completely different points of view. As is generally true, the path of wisdom is found in refusing to choose between the couch and the altar, but rather in *combining* the healing efforts of the ministers and the counselors, of the counseling room and of the altar.

To take this point even further, I want to emphasize that the psychology associated with the ministry of counseling is not foreign to the Bible and the Christian faith. I do not believe that psychology ought to be integrated with our Christian faith. To me this implies a forced union of two incompatibles by an act of misused intelligence or compromise. *Whatever* is true has its source in Christ, who said, "I am the truth." And in his letter to the church in Colosse Paul declared that in Christ "are hid all the treasures of wisdom and knowledge" (Col. 2:3). If psychology is the truth as it relates to the proper understanding of man, then it is not something *brought into* the Christian's world view. Rather it should be recognized as *belonging to* Christianity as wet belongs to water, as discernment belongs to wisdom, as love belongs to marriage.

How Does Counseling Help?

Often people ask, "Just how does counseling help?" The answer first requires a definition of counseling. When my clients ask me to explain counseling, I usually begin with what it is *not*. For example, counseling is not something done *to* you. This idea views the client as passively receiving "treatment," and mistakenly presumes a certain helplessness on the part of the client.

Second, counseling is not something done *for* you. This idea puts all the responsibility on the therapist, or helper, and prevents the client from accepting the proper role. Such an attitude, if put in words, says, "Here I am; now do something to solve my problems."

Counseling is better understood as something done *with* you. A counseling relationship is established when an invitation is accepted, when there is mutual willingness to give and receive gifts—trust, respect, understanding, self-disclosure. A fascinating explanation of counseling has been given by Dr. Paul Tournier, perhaps the world's most well-known Christian counselor. People travel from all over the world to consult with him in his home in Switzerland. When asked how he counsels people, Dr. Tournier replied, "I am very embarrassed by all these people who ask me that. I don't know how to help people. I don't do anything at all. What is important is that the people try to find their way and that I try to understand, to support them, to welcome them. What is important is that people find me a true friend, someone in whom they can confide everything. That is the most magnificent thing to see. What a privilege to find someone in whom you can confide without fear of being judged."

Counseling is the solution to our solitariness. Unanswered questions, unspoken fears and desires that disturb lead to a condition of loneliness. As this condition grows, the need to be known by another who can form a relationship that provides acceptance, understanding, and sincere caring becomes critical. Many kinds of problems have a socially alienating effect. This was David's feeling when he wrote, "I looked on my right hand, and beheld, but there was no man that would know me: refuge failed me; no man cared for my soul" (Ps. 142:4). "There was no man that would know me. . . ."

Gradually, we are helped through gaining confidence, learning better ways of finding, knowing, and using appropriate resources, and developing hope.

Resistance to Receiving Help

Earlier in this book I discussed some resistances to seeking help. Now I need to describe those resistances to receiving help once a helper has been found.

As amazing as it may seem, much counseling is struggling for clients against their wishes! It seems hard to believe that we can seek help and resist it at the same time. "Do you want to get well?" was the question Jesus asked a man who had been ill for thirty-eight years! Physical as well as psychological problems can serve purposes so rewarding that resistance to their elimination can be built up and stubbornly maintained. How we resist the truth when it doesn't please us! The Spanish philosopher Unamuno once claimed that "people want to be praised, amused, and deceived," adding that "sooner or later they may end by scorning and rebuffing their flatterers, entertainers, and deceivers."

We can begin with a widely-known type of resistance—resistance to growth. Understood in the biblical framework, growth means change in a Christ-approved direction. Such change can be desired and resisted at the same time. For change involves the person in behaving in new ways that can be very uncomfortable, even fearful. Every change has two movements: moving away from what has to be given up and moving toward what needs to be developed. And these movements generate insecurity, self-denial, struggle, and some failure—all of which can produce anxiety.

Second, we resist the disclosure of uncomplimentary truth about the way we feel, or what we have done or wanted to do.

A third resistance can be directed toward the helper.

Sometimes certain responses are expected from the helper but what the client gets is something very different. Disappointment, anger, resentment, or combinations of all these can result in resisting the helper's future attempts to assist.

Also, we have a tendency to resist giving up the advantages gained by certain behaviors, no matter how sinful or immature they may be.

Another resistance is commonly experienced during the period of strenuously working through problems. Old habits do not easily yield to change. As the proverb puts it: "Habits start out as cobwebs and end up as cables."

In addition, it is possible to resist getting better because a person may believe that he should suffer for wrongdoing. In many minds there exists a strong relationship between misconduct and suffering. A guilt-ridden conscience can be relieved by self-inflicted suffering that gives the person the feeling that he is paying for his sins.

Furthermore, there is resistance based on not wanting to become dependent on the helper. It can be damaging to a person's pride to admit a lack of self-sufficiency.

Finally, there is resistance that comes from the efforts of the devil. How deceived we are to believe that he doesn't exist! The apostle Paul was never more serious than when he warned the Christians at Ephesus that "we wrestle not against flesh and blood, but against principalities, against powers, against the rulers of darkness of this world, against spiritual wickedness in high places" (Eph. 6:12).

Resisting help can also be understood as a consequence of lack of knowledge; of unrealistic fears, which is to say wrong information; and of childhood experiences that produced harmful attitudes. Learning the wrong things leads to forming attitudes that create problems in relating to authority figures, peers, or mates. Attitudes formed by experiences in childhood can be very difficult to change, because those attitudes tend to produce effects that prove they are "right." For example, Carla's father made improper advances toward her. This gave her a negative attitude toward men. Her feelings of distrust and resentment cause her to behave toward men in ways that result in their negative response to her. When this happens she experiences a confirmation of her expectations. And with each confirmation the attitude becomes stronger.

How to Profit from Counseling

When you go to a medical doctor and he needs to give you a thorough physical examination he says, "Please remove your clothes. I'll be right back." If, when he returns, you still have your clothes on, the doctor will want to know, "Do you want me to help you, or not?" It's the patient's choice, isn't it? And it will be made according to how badly he wants help. The hang-up over undressing may be there, but if the desire for help is greater than the hang-up, the patient will undress as the doctor instructed.

In the same way, people bring all sorts of fears to the consulting room. But before the counselor can help them, they have to take their psychological clothes off—they have to be honest with the counselor, not holding anything back.

Many years of counseling experience have taught me that this kind of "unveiling" of the self is extremely rare because it's extremely difficult. Revealing the naked body to the physician may be a problem for many, but revealing the naked truth to a counselor is a problem for everyone!

Undoubtedly the major reason some people fail to benefit from counseling is that they withhold truth from the counselor. What they receive from him is based on what they revealed. Partial and/or false knowledge results in severely limiting the counselor's ability to identify the cause(s) of the client's problem(s). And when the cause is not identified, the remedy cannot be given.

In all of us there is the tendency to avoid facing any truth that does not agree with our opinion of ourselves. We can benefit by being aware of the avoidance strategies so regrettably common to us all.

Rationalization. When we give a socially acceptable (face-saving) reason for the real one, we are rationalizing. In his autobiography Benjamin Franklin wrote, "So convenient a thing it is to be a reasonable creature, since it enables one to find or make a reason for everything one has a mind to do."

Projection. When we are unwilling to recognize our personal sins, faults, and imperfections, and instead see them in others, we are projecting. This strategy makes us feel better personally by this favorable comparison. For example, Carl once participated in homosexual activity with his friend. As the years passed he became increasingly inclined to suspect others of being homosexual.

Denial. We deny the presence of a problem when we behave as though the problem does not exist. This behavior involves disguising the problem so that it can be avoided, which means that true feelings, attitudes, and faults are not acknowledged. Unfortunately, because of this pattern, persons who need help the most are often the last ones to recognize it!

Repression. This term describes the process by which we rid the conscious mind of disturbing thoughts and memories. Repressing problems does not eliminate them. This avoidance strategy makes connecting the cause of a problem with its consequences very difficult, and sometimes impossible without help.

Reaction formation. This means we conceal our true feelings behind a false front that gives the opposite impression. Shakespeare suggested that a person can protest "too much." A trained observer suspects reaction formation when someone "overdoes it" in denying a sinful, negative desire or in defending a positive one.

Psychosomatic reaction. This produces a physical symptom caused by a nonphysical problem. Nothing so effectively enables a person to avoid responsibility as being ill. Often the type of "illness" is related to the loss of function for which the person feels inadequate.

Displacement. This is a substitution of a less threatening goal for the original. For example, Bill is "told off" by his boss. He wants to fight back but fears losing his job. Instead he goes home and vents his anger by "telling off" his wife. She becomes Bill's scapegoat, the innocent target of his displaced anger.

Frequently people ask, "What is the difference between counseling and psychotherapy?" Admittedly there is a lot of jargon in psychology that confuses the general public. (And over the years I've discovered that not a little confusion exists among the professionals!) Every effort to understand the answer to this question will be most rewarding if we give careful consideration to some highly relevant Scripture: "Encourage one another and build each other up" (1 Thess. 5:11, NIV). Note the word *build* as it is used in the verse. What does a wise builder know and do? He uses the proper material. He realizes that his work will take time and require much effort. And he knows that if he goes according to the blueprint and does what he can each day, one day at a time, that eventually his building will be completed. By persisting with wisdom and patience the builder accomplishes the desired result.

Now think of counseling as building a life. Our blueprint is the Bible. Our materials include a relationship with the living Christ through the ministry of the Holy Spirit, prayer, regular public worship, and sharing our faith. Christian counseling takes the person where he is and begins the building process. My position is that psychotherapy is a special kind of building, requiring special

training and experience. Obviously some kinds of problems will require a special kind of knowledge on the part
of the counselor. And sometimes it is not easy to find the
right kind of help. But the Christian can be reassured by
the words of Christ, who promised, "Ask, and it shall be
given you; seek, and ye shall find; knock, and it shall be
opened unto you" (Matt. 7:7). As a member of the body
of Christ, you have access to the resources placed in the
body for your benefit. Learn to make use of them and
experience the help we all need as we build together. No
personal problem, no matter how impossible its solution
may seem at the moment, is beyond the resources of our
heavenly Father who manifested himself in Jesus Christ.

The most urgent kind of help comes to us in the form
of an infinitely precious gift. "For God so loved the
world, that he gave his only begotten Son, that whoso-
ever believeth in him should not perish, but have everlasting life" (John 3:16). Until this gift of Christ is
received, the solutions to personal problems are like
band-aids covering the measles. The heart of the problems is the problem of the heart, and until the heart is
made right nothing will be an adequate answer. This is
not a new discovery but comes from ancient wisdom.
King Solomon, the wisest man in the world of his day,
wrote, "Keep thy heart with all diligence; for out of it
are the issues of life" (Prov. 4:23). As we have seen, the
word *heart* denotes the deepest center of human personality, where our intentions, motives, and desires origi-
nate. For as the wise king knew, out of it—that is, the
heart—are the issues of life.

Behind all help is the Helper whose will is our highest
good and whose way is our greatest joy. Whatever another person is able to do that helps us to live better
should be understood in a way that strengthens our relationship to the loving source of that help. To continue
throughout the remainder of our lives to develop this
kind of understanding brings the insight described by the

psalmist: "Thou wilt shew me the path of life: in thy presence is fulness of joy; at thy right hand there are pleasures for evermore" (Ps. 16:11).

Professional Associations

Alcoholics Anonymous, P.O. Box 1980, Grand Central Annex, New York, NY 10017

American Association of Retired Persons, 1225 Connecticut Avenue, N. W., Washington, DC 20036

American Institute of Family Relations, 5287 Sunset Boulevard, Los Angeles, CA 90027

American Medical Association, 535 North Dearborn Street, Chicago, IL 60610

American Social Health Association, 1740 Broadway, New York, NY 10019

Association for Family Living, 6 North Michigan Avenue, Chicago, IL 60602

Auxiliary Council to the Association for the Advancement of Psychoanalysis, 329 East 62nd Street, New York, NY 10021

Child Study Association of America, 9 East 89th Street, New York, NY 10028

Child Welfare League of America, Inc. (adoption), 44 East 23rd Street, New York, NY 10010

Division of Publication Documents, U. S. Government Printing Office, Washington, DC 20402

Family Enrichment Bureau, 1615 Ludington Street, Escanaba, MI 49829

Family Life Publications, Inc., P. O. Box 427, Saluda, NC 28773

Family Service Association of America, 44 East 23rd Street, New York, NY 10010

Foster Parents Plan, Inc., 352 Park Avenue, South, New York, NY 10010

LeLeche League (expectant and new mothers), 9696 Minneapolis Avenue, Franklin Park, IL 60131

Maternity Center Association, 48 East 92nd Street, New York, NY 10028

National Association for Mental Health, Inc., 10 Columbus Circle, New York, NY 10019

National Association for Retarded Children, 2709 Avenue E., East, Arlington, TX 76011

National Easter Seal Society for Crippled Children and Adults, 2023 West Ogden Avenue, Chicago, IL 60612

National Rehabilitation Association, 1522 K Street, N. W., Washington, DC 20005

Natural Family Planning Association, P. O. Box 250, New Haven, CT 06502

Parents Without Partners Association, 80 Fifth Avenue, New York, NY 10003

U. S. Department of Health, Education, and Welfare, 330 Independence Avenue, S. W., Washington, DC 20201

This list is not exhaustive, nor does the inclusion of a group mean that the author endorses the views or goals of it.

Epilogue

As we come to the end of our present study, it is instructive to consider some of this book's implications.

One of the most promising trends of our time is that of renewed interest in the whole person. When man is understood in terms of spirit, mind, and body, the implications for spiritual development, education, medical science, behavioral science, and related disciplines become exciting indeed. Uncompromising commitment to scriptural truth combined with continued striving for excellence in research, development, implementation, and evaluation will lead us to discoveries that will enrich, expand, and heal beyond our previous experiences.

This deeper understanding of the whole person is already showing up in important ways. For the concerns dealt with in this book, perhaps our greatest emphasis should be on the greater responsibility we need to be taking for ourselves. Biblical insights in creative association with the best scientific evidence encourages increasing rejection of the concept of the person as being merely passive in favor of more responsible, mature, and disciplined patterns of Christian living.

We are not simply "patients" (to whom something is done). We are *persons* who can make enlightened responses that can enhance our lives, no matter what our problems are.

For example, we know that music is one of the greatest influences on emotion. Modern technological advances are providing affordable, high-quality Christian music on cassette tapes and records to which we can choose to listen, thereby experiencing positive effects emotionally. The Bible, good books (especially poetry), art, and disciplined use of the media can be utilized to contribute to correcting and stabilizing negative emotional conditions.

As members of the body of Christ we should be praying for wisdom and understanding regarding biblical and scientific insights into the nature, purpose, function, and interaction of the emotions, will, imagination, reason, and body.

A subject of particular concern in our time is stress, not only because of its presence in our lives now, but also because it will continue to increase in the future. Learning to understand it and to keep it at manageable levels in a world of increasing conflict and tension is a challenge that thinking Christians must recognize and confront.

Living sensitively, responsibly, and compassionately in our kind of world is neither simple nor easy. Human suffering and conflict, crime, wars, famine, disasters, disease, problems of every kind scream at us daily on our television sets, in our newspapers, and in other media. How much of this kind of tragic life can we allow ourselves to feel without becoming emotionally unbalanced ourselves? On the other hand, how much of this can we refuse to allow ourselves to feel without becoming calloused and insensitive?

An ancient Greek legend tells about a woman who came to be ferried to the region of departed spirits. She was reminded by Charon, the ferryman, that if she so desired she could drink of the waters of Lethe, thereby forgetting the life she was leaving. Her immediate response was, "I will forget how I've suffered." "And," Charon added, "you will forget how you have rejoiced." The woman continued, "I will forget my failures." The old ferryman said, "And also your victories." She said, "I will forget how I have been hated." "And," said Charon, "also how you have been loved." Recognizing the wise old ferryman's point, the woman decided not to drink Lethe's water, choosing to keep the memory of her sorrows, defeats, and disappointments rather than to give up the memory of her victories, joys, and loves.

As disciples of Christ, positioned in him, persuaded by him, and progressing for him, we seek not the narcotic effect of our secular society's Lethean water. Rather we choose to live in growing fellowship with Christ who never leaves us nor forsakes us. One of our challenges in this regard is to learn that we don't lose our belief in the miraculous as we gain in understanding of the patterns it takes requiring insight, time, and effort. Such an undertaking focuses biblically on principle, parables, paradox, priority, and perspective. Serious attention will need to be given to the words *discipline, duty, commitment, character, responsibility, holiness, perseverance, absolutes.*

Too much is at stake for us to fail to grow in our understanding of the relationship of emotional health to other kinds of health—physical, mental, and spiritual. The families, churches, schools, clinics, hospitals, businesses, and political leaders making the greatest contributions to our society in the future will succeed in making this relationship ever more clear.

The goal that we hope to achieve has been expressed best by the apostle Paul, who said, "I have learned to find resources in myself whatever my circumstances. . . . I have been very thoroughly initiated into the human lot with all its ups and downs. . . . I have strength for anything through him who gives me power" (Phil. 4:11–13, NEB).